AGES
and
STAGES

**DEVELOPMENTAL DESCRIPTIONS & ACTIVITIES
BIRTH THROUGH EIGHT YEARS**

Written and illustrated by
KAREN MILLER

International Standard Book Number 0–910287–05–8

Library of Congress Cataloging in Publication Data

Miller, Karen, 1942-
  Ages & stages

    Bibliography: p.
    1. Child development. 2. Sensory stimulation.
I. Title. II. Title: Ages and stages.
RJ131.M54   1985   155'.4   85-25175
ISBN 0-910287-05-8

0-910-287-05-8

Written and Illustrated by Karen Miller

NINTH PRINTING   NOVEMBER 1997

Table of Contents

Contents

Contents

Dedication

I dedicate this book to Polly McVickar. In years of teaching at her Malibu home, "Imagination Mountain," for Pacific Oaks College, she emphasized the value of stretching the imaginative thinking powers of children and adults through experiences in literature, art, music and science. More than anything, Polly emphasizes the wonderful uniqueness of each human being.

Acknowledgements

This volume represents information and insights gained from 15 years of observing children and teachers in child care situations all over the country. If I had only my own personal resources and experiences to draw on, there would be no book. I would like to express my personal gratitude especially to the teachers of Children's World, Inc. who have allowed me to stare at them, take pictures of them, and pick their brains for the last six years.

In the process of writing this I had invaluable specific advice and input from the following Master Teachers of Children's World: Tammy Notter of Bolingbrook, Ill., Lauri Maltby of Livonia, Michigan, Mary McHugh of St. Paul, Minnesota, Terri Santi of Arvada, Colorado, Pat Henkel of Westlake, California, Marta Sanchez of Rowland Heights, California, and Kathy Setter of Minneapolis, Minnesota.

I want to give very special thanks to Diane Barclay of Seattle, WA for helping me conceptualize the entire book, and giving a great deal of actual input on early drafts.

Introduction

Caring for young children is work full of challenges, rewards and surprises. It is the "surprises" part that keeps us interested. Watching young children grow and develop new skills is one of the most rewarding parts of being a parent or a teacher. Keeping children interested and happily occupied while they are learning requires that we know them well.

The primary focus of this book is on how developmental stages and behaviors show up in group child care situations. My remarks and observations are confined to that type of setting. I do not talk about such things as bedtime rituals, sibling rivalry and other issues confined mainly to family situations. Recognizing that every parent is part teacher, and every teacher must "parent" children, it is hoped that parents as well as teachers will find information of value in these pages.

This book is intended to let you know what you can expect of "typical" children of various ages ... what their capabilities, understandings and interests are. Please be aware that there is a wide variation in abilities and behaviors of "normal" children. Do not be alarmed if a particular child does not match a description exactly.

If you work with young children you need to understand the concept of "emerging skills." Emerging skills are capabilities, both physical and mental, that children are just about to be able to do, or have just recently mastered. The interesting thing is that when a skill is new like this, it is usually "compulsive." Children want to do it again and again and again. This "self-imposed drill" seems to be a natural learning style for humans.

An easy to recognize emerging skill is when a baby of about 8 or 9 months learns to pull up to a standing position, holding on to some stable object such as a crib rail or sofa edge. At first the child may not know how to get back down and will cry. The adult will go over and help the child get back down to a sitting position again. Then right away, what does the child do? He pulls back up to a standing position! You see an emerging skill in the baby who loves to crawl up stairs, the toddler who first learns to walk, the two year old who learns to name objects, the three year old who learns to cut with scissors, the four year old who learns to ride a low-slung tricycle, the five year old who starts to read words. Incidentally, this phenomenon is not limited to children. Think of the teen-ager who learns to drive a car, or the adult who learns how to ski.

In planning your program, the trick is to zero in on the emerging skills of the children in your group. Even in closely matched age groups, you will find a lot of variation in children's capabilities and interests. How do you plan activities that will meet the needs of all cf them? First of all, many activities and materials, playdough for instance, have a fairly broad range of appeal. Children will use the same materials with different levels of skill and complexity. Secondly, you can set up an environment with many choices of acceptable activities for children. Then you must *trust children* to go to the activity they need at that time to feed their emerging skills. You will find children who, left to their own devices, will choose to play in the block corner, or the dress up corner, or paint at the easel again and again for weeks at a stretch. That tells you that these activites are satisfying some essential learning need in the child. As a teacher, you can add variety to these activities, bringing in different props, varying the material slightly, and playing with the children from time to time, expanding on their play and helping them build upon their ideas.

Presenting good group activities is a special challenge for caregivers. If most of the children squirm and have trouble paying attention, it is a signal to you that you have "missed the mark" and the activity is either too difficult or too simple for children, or perhaps it is presented in a way that makes it hard for them to concentrate. If one child gets up and wanders around (common with younger children) it's usually best to allow this to happen, especially if there is another adult in the room to keep an eye on him or her.

You will quickly learn to simplify or add difficulty to an activity or toy. Are there too many words in the book? Turn the pages and simply "tell" the story, rather than reading it, adjusting the vocabulary to the level of the children in front of you. Is the puzzle too simple? Ask the child to try to put it together with eyes closed. Don't hesitate to end an activity that doesn't hold children's attention . . . stay flexible.

This is not a "curriculum book." When I include specific ideas, they are meant to give you an example of the type of activity that will promote the skill being discussed. These activities will be indented and in italics. They should be used as "starting points" to develop your own variations. Furthermore, I will not tell you, for instance, that by the time the child is four she should know the following things, and then go about listing them. It's just not that simple. A lot will depend on your values and what goals your own program chooses to identify.

Since there is such an interest in early academics, I have endeavored to summarize at the end of chapters what "pre-reading" involves for the age being discussed.

I encourage you to read the chapter before and the chapter after the age group you are working with as well as that particular chapter. Some children may be advanced in physical skills and behind in language, or the other way around. It is always good to know where the child is coming from and where he is headed when looking at the current level of development. In child care situations children are rarely grouped the way the chapters are divided in this book. There are often three and a half year olds and young fours in the same group, for instance. Remember that growth is a continuum. A child doesn't suddenly stop being "two" and start being "three" on her third birthday.

All through the book, I have taken the liberty of listing some of my personal favorite resource books on given topics. There are a great many others.

A note on terminology: I use the words "teacher" and "caregiver" interchangeably to indicate adults working with children. I will refer to children randomly in both the masculine and feminine gender.

This book is not meant to be a guide to identify children with developmental delays or special needs. If you suspect a child in your group is seriously outside the "norm" for his or her age, it is best to confer with parents and have the child observed by someone with special training.

It is also not the purpose of this book to have you "teach" skills at an earlier age . . . that would be like trying to teach children to get taller! Children grow according to their own inner time table. The rate at which they develop skills does not necessarily correlate with a child's intelligence. Although the rate of development varies from child to child, the "pattern" or "order" in which they learn skills and develop characteristics is quite consistent. In other words, the "ages" part varies, but the "stages" part is consistent. It is also important to focus on the "whole child," the emotional and social development as well as the intellectual and physical development.

By understanding what to expect of the children in your group and respecting their own innate drive to learn and develop, you can plan your program to present just the right challenge for children and not be frustrating or boring. That allows children to develop their optimum potential. Stay tuned-in to your children, and enjoy them for the unique individuals that they are!

CHAPTER 1

Birth To Six Months

Lucky is the person who gets to spend time around these youngest children. You see more than anybody, the miracle of a new life, a developing person. Although much of an infant's time is spent sleeping or being fed and diapered, there is still time to play, cuddle and enjoy learning about what it means to be alive.

As a caregiver of young infants, you have a very important role. From you, parents, and close family members, the baby is learning what it is to be a human being. The caregiver of infants needs to be a very warm and responsive person, and able to interpret a baby's cries and gurglings. The baby needs your body to cling to.

You also need to be well organized, keeping track of feeding and sleeping needs, good at keeping written records, and confident and relaxed in communicating with parents.

Your most important responsibility is to keep the infant safe and physically comfortable, and in a group care situation, this sometimes means protecting the baby from older, inquisitive children.

Recent research is discovering that babies in the first half year of life have many more capabilities than was previously thought. There is much you can do to help the baby have a good time when she is awake.

Emotional

"Bonding" and "basic trust" are the basics for human emotional development that have their roots in early infancy.

Bonding

A "bond" is the instinctive strong attachment of human and animal babies to their mothers. The instinctive bond to the mother comes first. This must be in place for normal emotional development to take place. It is important to understand that this doesn't necessarily have to be the biological mother. In cases where the biological mother is not available because of sickness, death, emotional illness, adoption or some other cause, a "primary caregiver" or "mothering one," can provide this bond. This could be a father or grandparent. This first human emotional attachment, though, is the starting point for all human relationships. Then the child can expand the circle to other human beings . . . at first just a few. That's why it is important not to have much staff turnover in an infant program, so that the child is cared for by one or two loving, caring, familiar adults.

Basic Trust

"Basic Trust" is the idea that the child learns that her needs will be met. She learns this by a rhythm of distress and relief. The child feels the distress of hunger and cries. The mother or caregiver hears the cry, comes and picks up the baby and feeds her. The distress is relieved. This pattern is repeated and consistent. When a child learns she can trust mother/caregiver to relieve her distress, the trust grows into a feeling of security, and later confidence to try new things. It is the basis for self-esteem.

The concept of basic trust is one good reason, among many others, that babies should be on a "demand" schedule rather than a schedule contrived for the convenience of adults. The child should sleep, be fed, be diapered, be cuddled and played with according to the child's own inner schedule. The caregiver must "tune-in" to the baby's signals.

Crying

People caring for infants should make every effort to pick up crying babies promptly and try to comfort them. In generations past there was the idea that picking up babies would "spoil" them and they should be left to "cry it out" so that they do not become demanding as they grow older. This notion has been proven untrue. In fact, babies who are picked up promptly and cared for in a very responsive way turn out to be more content and compliant in the second half of their first year and later toddlerhood. This is one good reason for low staff/child ratios in infant centers.

It is instinctively distressing to adults to hear a crying baby. Often a baby's cry will be relieved by feeding or diapering. But at times this is not enough. Sometimes the caregiver will have fed, diapered, and "burped" a baby, and determined that the child is not feverish or otherwise ill, and the child will still cry. Other ways to comfort the new baby are walking with the baby, rocking, singing, and giving the child a pacifier. Interestingly, babies often seem to respond best to fast, little rocks — about 60 beats per minute. Perhaps it is because this approximates the mother's heart beat. Babies should be held close and comforted, even if they continue to cry. Your mere presence is offering sympathy.

It is not appropriate to talk about "discipline" concerning young babies. Infants in their first year do not willfully misbehave to vex adults. They do not have the experience or mental systems to understand cause and effect relationships and what makes others mad. It is when adults misunderstand this that the most tragic instances of abuse of infants occur. Babies cry because of some physical distress or pain or fear, not to annoy.

Sucking

Sucking is a great need for babies under a year, and especially for newborns. If a child is fortunate enough to locate her own thumb, fingers or fist to suck on, by all means allow it. A pacifier can bring welcome comfort to a fretful baby, and is not considered harmful by doctors, if you keep it clean.

Social

The newborn baby is usually pretty "sober" when awake and not crying. However, she will stare intently at a human face around 8 to 12 inches from her eyes. She is definitely interested in people.

Feeding

Getting fed is the most important thing that happens in a baby's day, especially from the baby's point of view. Not only is she getting nourishment, she is absorbing all the "nurturing"— the holding, and cuddling and body contact — and developing some basic attitudes about food, and bodies, for that matter. A baby should always be held when fed.

With some new babies, their digestive system doesn't work well, and they experience a lot of gastric distress. A colic condition can last up to three months. Introducing new foods can also cause some distress. For this reason, new food should always be introduced by parents at home, preferably on a weekend to see how the child tolerates it.

Communicate closely with parents about what the baby should have to eat and drink. Most babies quickly establish a "routine" of regular intervals when they are hungry. Knowing each baby's routine will help you plan your day . . . but remember to listen to the child's signals rather than just watching the clock. All day care situations for infants should have specific procedures for keeping written records of when, what and how much an infant ate. Your state child care licensing agency also spells out how food must be stored. Be sure to make yourself aware of these guidelines and regulations.

Feeding Position

Always hold the baby in your arms, close to your body as you feed her. She can feel secure in your warm embrace, and look intently into your eyes. Eating is a social activity from the very beginning.

Smiling

It is at around 6 weeks of age that the child develops that irresistible genuine social smile that warms the heart of any adult who is the lucky recipient. A baby will usually smile at almost any face that appears about one foot away from her eyes. Perhaps this is why adults naturally put their faces close to babies when they talk to them.

Then at about 3 months comes that wonderful belly-laugh and joyful excitement.

"Ah-Boo"

This is the game that people have been playing with babies, "by instinct" since time began. Place the child on your lap in front of you. Smile and say "Ah-boo" as you lean toward the baby and gently bump your forehead to the baby's. Repeat this as long as the activity seems enjoyable to the baby.

General Contact Play

Give the child access to your body. When the child starts to have some head control, lie down on the floor and put the baby on your chest, letting her reach for your nose, grab your hair, and look into your face.

Hold the baby up over your head and gaze into each other's faces and coo.

Take advantage of diapering time for easy social interactions like this.

Visual Development

A baby's social development is affected by his growing ability to see faces, colors and movement. The vision of a newborn is much sharper than once thought. The baby will look into the eyes of the person holding him. A new baby will also stare at a drawing of the upper half of a human face when it is placed 6" to 12" away.

Crib Face

You could place a picture of a face with well defined eyes and eyebrows on the right side (since most babies have their head turned to the right about 85% of the time) of the baby's crib. When the baby is awake she may enjoy staring at the face.

Babies are also visually attracted to bright colors and sharp contrasts.

Pattern Cards

Make some cards about 8" square, with bright, bold patterns on them. These could be placed at the side of the crib for the baby to look at, or you could hold them in front of the baby momentarily while you are holding her. See if they attract her attention.

Pattern Mobile

You could make a crib mobile that hangs about 18" above the baby and off to the right side. Design it so the baby, not primarily the adult sees the pattern of the things that hang . . . in other words, have the things hanging horizontally rather than vertically. Rather than hanging cute little animals and the like, hang cards with some bold patterns, which the baby will find much more interesting.

Infants are attracted by things that move and can follow them with their eyes. That is one reason mobiles that jiggle or rotate are interesting. When the child is 6 weeks old she becomes skillful at following moving objects with her eyes, and can focus on all distances.

Tracking

Place the baby on her back on the floor. Hold a bright object about 12 inches over her head and jiggle it to get her attention. Then move the object from side to side slowly, and allow the baby to follow the object with her eyes. She may show excitement and move her arms and legs. How long will this keep her interest?

Mirror

Attach an unbreakable mirror to the wall sideways at floor level. A baby in an infant seat will enjoy gazing at her reflection. An older baby who can hold her head up will be entertained lying on her stomach in front of the mirror. A low mirror will remain interesting to all stages of infants.

Hold the baby upright on your shoulder some of the time so the baby can look around the room.

Language

Of course, young babies do not produce or understand words. What they are finding out is that when they produce noises, they'll get some action. So they are seeing the beginnings of language as a means to an end . . . getting your needs met. Basic communication. After about 2 months they will also enjoy gurgling and making noises with their saliva.

By all means, talk to babies (you'll only sound crazy to other adults!). You are giving a baby a "feel" for language. By the way, "baby talk" where the adult raises his or her voice and eyebrows, and says silly sounding words, is just fine for babies. Babies seem to respond best to this type of speech. Happy chatter, singing, and laughter enhance the atmosphere of the room, and the child picks up on moods.

Music

Lullabies have been used since the beginning of time to comfort babies. *Live* singing from someone holding you is a wonderful gift for a baby. They feel the vibrations of your body as they hear the sounds. They are learning part of the human repertoire. It doesn't matter at all, of course, whether you can hold a tune or not. A baby room with singing in it is a nice place to be.

Physical

Tonic Neck Reflex

Newborns up to the age of about 6 weeks are bound by the "Tonic neck reflex" which is a common position for babies. When you place the baby on her back, her head will go to one side or the other, usually the right side. Arms and legs will usually take on the "fencer's pose." The arm on the side that the baby's head is facing will be stretched out. The other arm will be bent at the elbow and the fist will be up. The leg on the side of the out-stretched arm will be bent at the knee. The other leg will be stretched out straight. If you gently turn the child's head to the other side, the arms and legs will change position accordingly.

Head Control and Mobility

Newborns cannot lift their heads. When you place them on their stomachs, a position which is often most comfortable for babies, their head will be to one side. Although the baby cannot roll over or move around, some babies, when angry, manage to propel their bodies the entire length of the crib by repeatedly digging their feet into the mattress surface and thrusting out with their legs. That is why a bumper pad placed around the edges of the crib is a good idea.

It is important always to provide head support when you lift or hold a new baby.

At about 6 or 8 weeks the baby lying on her back can move her head from side to side, and is often seen with knees bent and both hands brought to the middle of her chest.

Startle Response

The "startle" response, common with newborns, often startles adults. The child who was lying quietly will suddenly jump or twitch. It is not cause for alarm. It is simply a sign of an immature nervous system.

Leg Thrusting

If you place something at the bottom of the feet of a baby of 6 or 8 weeks of age she is likely to kick out against it. Held upright with feet against the floor, the baby may thrust out legs against the floor.

When the baby is 3 months old she will greatly enjoy making powerful leg thrusts when lying on her back.

Foot Gong

Try holding a cookie sheet at the feet of a 3 month old for her to bang her feet against.

Head and Torso Control

It is around 6 weeks of age that a baby first starts to lift her head and look around when placed on her stomach. By 3 months she's getting pretty good at it.

At about 3 or 4 months the baby is getting more torso control and may even roll over before long. Place the child on a clean blanket on the floor when she is awake so she can practice twisting and moving her body.

Infant seats were designed for babies who cannot yet sit by themselves. The incline allows the child to watch what is going on around the room.

Small bean bag chairs are also comfortable, stable seats for babies, providing stability and good torso support.

Hands

1. Fists

A new baby's hands are closed in tight fists. If you pry the fingers open and put your finger across the palm of her hand, the baby's fingers will close tightly around your finger. This is why new babies can hold onto a rattle. The rattle will not have any meaning for the baby though, and she may even bang herself in the face with it.

Some babies become successful at getting their fists into their mouths to suck on.

2. Discovering Hands

At about 6 weeks the baby's hands will relax more and start to open. It is at this stage when the child is lying on her back she will suddenly notice her hands moving across her field of vision. What a fascinating discovery! The child will spend a lot of time staring at her hands, and discover that she has some control over those funny moving things!

Hand Mitts

Some caregivers make little "mitts" from baby socks with holes cut in them for fingers to stick out. With bright colors or faces on them, these make hands even more interesting to look at.

3. Batting

When the child is about 2 months old she may start swiping or batting at interesting objects dangled overhead. This is the time to take flimsy mobiles out of cribs and replace them with sturdy "crib gyms" designed for children to grab and pull on. Make sure the objects are securely attached.

Target Practice

Hold a toy that makes an interesting noise over the child's head when the child is in an infant seat or lying on the floor. Jiggle it to get the child to bat at it. (The child will also enjoy kicking at this).

4. Grasping

At four months, when an object is placed in a child's hand, she is likely to look at it and bring it to her mouth to be gummed. At about 4 months the baby may actually succeed in grabbing something. It won't be easy though. She is not yet good at opening her hand before she makes contact with the object, and her aim is fairly random.

Discovering Feet

Not long after the child discovers her hands, she discovers her feet! Wow . . . neat! When the baby is lying on her back her knees are often bent with her feet sticking straight up. Interesting visual targets they make as they move around up there. Soon the child will grasp her feet and hang on, enjoying feeling the dynamics of her own body.

The Play Environment for Babies

An environment for infants should include a clean, carpeted floor space where an adult can sprawl out comfortably with a baby. Some state licensing regulations require the presence of a playpen, not for confining babies, but for protecting them. A young infant can be placed inside a playpen for a few minutes while the adult cannot be right next to him, and be relatively safe from the curious advances of older infants and toddlers.

Interesting pictures and patterns can be attached to vertical surfaces for children in infant seats to look at. Have an assortment of interesting objects for babies to hold and examine and put in their mouths. Naturally, be careful that they are safe, and can be washed and kept clean.

Be conscious of fatigue on the part of the baby. They can tolerate only so much stimulation. After you have dangled an object for a baby to look at or swipe at for a few minutes, you may notice the baby look away. You can play "A-boo!" only so many times before it becomes tiring. Each child will have a different threshold for all play activities, so remain sensitive to their signals.

Focus

In caring for infants between birth and 6 months, concentrate not so much on "teaching" as on providing a warm, nurturing environment. Responsibilities fall into three major areas:

1. Responsive Care

The most important thing in the first six months of life is *good, responsive, physical care* of babies. Now, this is really saying a lot, especially since we include the word, "responsive."

Responsive means staying tuned in to the baby's cues, picking up and comforting promptly, and allowing the baby to sleep, eat and be changed according to her own rhythms. Young babies also need to be protected from curious older babies. Lots of holding, cuddling and loving attention!

2. Record Keeping and Communication

There's a lot of paper work in a good infant center. And it is extremely important to maintain good, close communications with parents, both face to face and in writing. You are not a substitute parent, you are a parent "support system." Earning a parent's "basic trust" is as important as gaining that from infants.

3. Stimulation

An environment for infants should have interesting things to look at and do during waking hours as skills develop. Use the activities described in this chapter as "starting points," adding your own variations.

CHAPTER 2

The Six To Eight Month Old

This is a baby who is really getting interesting. Up to now it has been a cute little bundle whose needs centered mainly around cuddling, a lot of physical contact and good, responsive physical care in the management of feeding, diapering and sleeping routines. Now we have a child who reaches, sits up, moves, and vocalizes in a most engaging way.

People who work with this age group need to be warm and "nurturing," able to interpret and respond to babies' grunts and non-verbal signals, and knowledgeable about setting up interesting things for babies to do.

Social-Emotional

The child between 6 and 8 months of age typically has a sunny disposition, as long as he is feeling well, although this may change once the child becomes mobile and is no longer content to just sit and look. Usually the child is friendly to almost anyone and smiles easily. He enjoys prolonged play with adults and is inclined to giggle a lot. It is possible, though, that as the child approaches 8 months he may become wary of strangers.

Get down on the floor and play with the baby. Hand the child toys and let him hand them back to you. Play peek-a-boo and laugh at each other. Let the child crawl over you and in and out of your lap. Enjoy and encourage his sociability.

Greet other people who enter the room with friendliness and openness while you are with the baby, providing a pro-social model for the child.

Like infants of an earlier age, these babies need very much to feel secure in the love of their caregivers. It is important for the caregiver to cuddle, hug, and generally rejoice in the child. Caring for infants of any age must be a love affair.

Physical

Rolling Over

Around the age of 6 months, sometimes earlier, sometimes later, the child will gain enough torso control to turn over from back to stomach and from stomach to back. It's really fun to watch the first few times the baby succeeds at this. There is an expression of startled surprise and amazed excitement on his face. And, of course, he wants to do it again!

There is no need to "teach" a child to roll over. It is one of those things he will learn to do by himself. All you have to do is provide him with the opportunity. When the child is awake, put him on a clean blanket on the floor, lying down on his back or stomach, perhaps with a few interesting objects around to reach for and handle.

Some babies enjoy rolling over so much that rolling becomes their prime means of getting from one place to another.

Sitting Up

Once the baby can roll over, sitting up is not far behind. It takes the ability to hold the head steady,, and torso control to maintain balance.

Small bean bag chairs are good "pre-sitting" devices because they support the child's torso. Children will start to lean forward and gradually gain more control.

When you sense that the child is just about ready to sit independently without being propped, let him gain experience in the safety of your lap on the floor. If you sit with your legs crossed and place the child in the middle with his back leaning against you, you provide a nice, soft base to fall back against. Your knees are there for support.

Next, let the child sit in the V of your legs directly on the floor.

Learning to sit up independently is a big step forward developmentally. The child sees the world from a new perspective and can spot things across the room.

When placed on the floor in a lying down position the child will often push himself up to a sitting position. With this new control of his posture, the child is itching to get at the rest of the world and come in contact with the enticing objects that are out of reach.

Leg Thrusts

If the child is held in an upright position with feet touching the floor, he will probably push his legs against the floor and enjoy bouncing up and down. The child is getting these leg muscles ready for walking.

Bounce chairs, wind-up swings and sturdy walkers are enjoyed by children this age, provided they are not over-used. These pieces of baby equipment have been controversial. There have been discussions of circulation problems, and putting too much pressure on bones not yet ready to hold the weight of the child. It will not hurt if children are in these things for short periods of time. The added mobility is exciting for the child, and boosts the growth of curiosity. Do not keep a child in a walker, swing, or bounce chair for extended periods of time. Remember, they need the floor time too, to develop coordination.

Creeping and Crawling

Crawling is defined as moving using the arms to pull the body along, with the abdomen on the floor.

Creeping is when the child moves on hands and knees with the abdomen above the floor.

A baby this age may start to crawl or "scooch" across the floor in some other way. The baby usually starts by trying to get at something just out of reach.

Place the child, lying down on his stomach, on a clean, carpeted floor with a number of interesting small toys in the area, some within reach, some just out of reach. By putting a few things out of reach, the child will be motivated to practice moving across a space.

The transition from crawling to creeping is fun to watch. The child will often "rock" back and forth on hands and knees without making progress, but enjoying the feeling. Some babies can't seem to get into forward gear, and mainly creep backwards. And there are occasionally babies who skip the creeping stage, going directly to pulling up and walking around holding onto things. This is fairly rare.

Make sure the baby has plenty of "free floor time" to gain experience crawling and creeping. They need the practice of making their arms and legs work together.

Texture Trail

> Gather variously textured materials to spread across your floor for children to crawl across. Carpet samples, hemp door mats, rubber door mats, astro-turf door mats, and throw rugs can be lined up to make an interesting "trail" for the child to follow. These things could be gathered up and put away, to be put out in a different arrangement each day.
>
> This can be done outside as well in a permanent way using natural materials such as wood slices, smooth stones embedded in concrete, pebbled concrete, sand, and bark.

Visually Directed Reaching

This baby is gaining skill at "visually directed reaching." That means looking at something within reach, opening his hand before it makes contact with the object and closing his fingers at the right time to grasp the object. A younger child could grasp things, but the timing of opening and closing fingers was not well-refined. Often the child would just bump or bat at objects and not actually get hold of them. Now the child can plan the action and carry it out. It is a major step in gaining control of the world.

Grab Board

Attach several attractive toys to sewing elastic and suspend them from a wall or sturdy partition of some sort. The child can try to grasp the objects. A not yet sitting up child could be placed within reach in an infant seat. You will be amazed at how challenging this is for children just learning the skill. It is almost frustrating for adults to watch. Make sure the toys are safe (too large to choke on, no sharp edges, etc.) because they will surely be put in the mouth. Also, make sure that the vertical surface they are attached to is very stable and could never be pulled over on the child.

Exploring Objects

Once the child gets good at visually directed reaching and can crawl around the room, the world is his to explore! The excitement is quite visible!

A child this age very much likes to examine small objects and toys, especially those that make a noise. He will typically hold an object with both hands and put it in his mouth. He will pass the object from one hand to the other and turn it around to see all sides. It will go into the mouth several times in the process. The child will also probably bang the object against a surface to see what kind of noise it makes. It is as if this junior scientist is making an investigation to find out all the possible properties and uses for this strange thing.

Shaker toys (rattles) are great for this age. Squeeze toys that squeak are fun, too.

A Shake-shake Collection

Make a collection of toys that make a noise when they are shaken. There are, of course, many ways to make these from cans with plastic lids and boxes. A coffee can with a clothespin inside will sound different from a spice can with grains of rice inside. The child will enjoy exploring the differences.

Make sure tops remain securely fastened so that the child does not swallow what's inside.

Children will enjoy this type of collection from now on through the toddler years.

Making the Environment Safe

All kinds of objects are interesting to children this age, not just toys. Small boxes, jar lids, keys, you name it. This is a good time to do a thorough "check" of your environment to make sure there are no dangerous things for a child to handle. Dangling cords from such things as irons at home and radios and clocks on shelves are hazards sometimes overlooked by adults. Make sure safety caps are inserted in all electrical outlets within reach of a crawling baby. Please read the more thorough discussion of this topic in the next chapter.

Language

This is the wonderful stage of babbling or "jargon" talk. The child will carry on, creating the most marvelous string of sounds, getting ready to utter his first words in months to come. In this critical stage of language development the child is practicing the sounds and intonations of his native language.

Talk a lot! Surround the child with meaningful language about what he is seeing in front of him. Describe everything that you are doing with him. Children learn to understand language much earlier than they learn to speak. You are providing a very important model for sounds and intonations while you are providing names for objects and actions.

When the child babbles and coos, answer him in like fashion. Try to imitate his sounds. This social child will undoubtedly enjoy the interchange, and you are modeling the give and take of conversation...(a skill many adults haven't seemed to master well!) The child is learning that language is a social tool as well as a means of getting what you want.

Music

When the baby babbles away is he talking or singing? Probably half of both. The child is really learning to use his voice in many different ways.

La, la, la

Try singing two or three notes over and over just saying "la" and see if the child comes close to imitating your chant.

If you sing a lot the child will learn that singing is one thing people do with their voices, and it is more likely to become part of his early repertoire of things to do with one's voice.

Object Permanence

One of the interesting developments toward the end of this stage is "object permanence." Up until now, if something left the baby's field of vision, it "ceased to exist" in the mind of the child. "Out of sight, out of mind." You can see this if you catch a younger child's attention with an attractive new object, just out of reach. Cover the object up, and the child will not try to look for it or remove the barrier between himself and the toy. When a child develops object permanence, he will try to pull away the covering to get at the object again.

Try this yourself. Show the child something very attractive, like a cookie, so that you are sure interest is high. Hide the cookie behind a piece of cardboard. Does the child knock the cardboard away to get at the cookie, or just lose interest and look away?

Developing object permanence is a very significant mental development. It means that the child can retain a mental image of an object that is not within sight. It is the very beginning of abstract thought . . . which is the basis for the development of imagination, fantasy play, and using symbols to represent objects, as in reading.

Like so many developments in the first years, object permanence is not something you must "teach" babies. It happens by itself... probably when the child's physical neurological development is at the right point. But once you recognize this as an "emerging skill" you can have lots of fun with it. There are many games playing with object permanence that children will enjoy... for quite a time to come, as well.

Peek-A-Boo Variations

1. Simply put your hands in front of your face, and remove them, saying "peek-a-boo!"

2. Pop up and down from behind a divider or piece of furniture.

3. Put a scarf over your head and pull it off, saying "peek-a-boo."

4. Put the scarf over the child's head and pull it off saying "peek-a-boo." Next, let the child pull the scarf off himself.

5. Have a stuffed animal or puppet play peek-a-boo.

6. Put stuffed animals inside boxes with lids for children to open and discover. Put the lid back on and say "Byebye." Uncover again... repeat.

7. Turning the pages of a book back and forth has a peek-a-boo appeal. Pictures disappear and reappear.

Focus

1. Responsive physical care. This baby still needs, most of all, a warm, loving, responsive adult... a personal relationship with a cherished caregiver.

2. Opportunities to move. In this time of major physical development, the child must have a chance to use his muscles. Babies who are awake should not be kept in cribs, but allowed to wiggle, roll and sit up on the floor.

3. Safe objects to look at, swipe at and examine. Make the infant's world an interesting place.

CHAPTER 3

The Eight To Fourteen Month Old

What an exciting age! It is the physical development that dominates everything in this stage. In this brief span of months the child moves from someone just able to scootch around the floor to someone who can *walk* and begin to explore the universe! What a daring accomplishment! With her newfound skill, this baby will need constant watching. It is the age of falling down, running into things, pulling on anything within reach, and sticking everything in the mouth. In spite of numerous minor injuries that seem to go with the age, the drive to walk is so strong that the child will get up and do it again and again until she drops from exhaustion.

The caregiver of this age child needs to be loving and responsive and prepared to give a long-term commitment. A lot of staff turnover can be very distressing to this age. This person must rejoice in the child's new accomplishments and encourage safe exploration. Above all, this teacher must be vigilant in supervising the child's safety, and have a high energy level.

Social-Emotional

Stranger Anxiety

Although not all children go through this, many babies who were formerly very open and accepting of new people, at about 8

25

months become frightened of new faces. Many a grandmother has been confused and disappointed at this reaction. Children will develop attachments to certain people — members of the immediate family and their primary caregivers, and nobody else better come near!

It's true that children in group child care situations experience less stranger anxiety than children cared for at home because they are used to many people coming in and out of the room, but stranger anxiety is by no means non-existent in child care.

This may be a particularly difficult time for a child to enter child care and experience a major change in her life. It will simply take patience and gentle understanding on the part of the caregiver, as well as compassion for the pain the child's distress causes parents. Eventually the child will develop trust in the caregiver and become attached to this new, familiar face.

Limit the number of people who come in and out of your room. It's true that parents of children in the room must enter and leave each day. It is probably wise not to allow a lot of other "visitors" such as college students who need to observe a baby, or volunteers, unless the volunteer can commit to be there on a regular, consistent basis every day.

When babies cry and cling to you in fear when strangers enter the room, do not force the child to go over to the stranger. It is probably best to ask costumed characters such as Santa Claus, clowns and the Easter Bunny, to skip your room when they make their visits to your center. Allow the child the security of your lap when a stranger is present. If the child feels safe, she may crawl down on her own and approach the stranger. It should be done on her own terms.

If you, the cherished caregiver, model friendliness to strangers coming in and out of the room and give enthusiastic greetings, the child will probably eventually copy your behavior.

With new children having trouble adjusting, it helps a great deal if the same caregiver receives the child from the parent every morning, and assumes primary responsibility for her during the day. The child must develop trust in one adult first before she can generalize her feeling of comfort to other people.

Pride

The child is making such exciting progress in physical abilities during this period. Mastering a new physical skill is very exciting. The child's face will show it. "Wow . . . I did it!!!" It's important for the adults in the child's life to share in this joy and excitement. "Look at you! You're standing up! You did it!" A round of applause is not inappropriate!

The adult's endorsement will give the child encouragement to go on trying new things. Basking in the approval of important adults is vital to the child's development of self-esteem and later psychological and intellectual development. Of course, this interest of adults is important all through childhood. Share in children's pride and excitement in their new accomplishments!

Setting Limits

This is an often difficult time for adults. It is important to let children explore the environment without a lot of "no's." We just talked about celebrating children's accomplishments. And yet, we know that we cannot let the child do whatever she wants and have general free run of the place. That would lead to toddler anarchy!

The best advice is to have an environment where much activity is "allowable." If the child starts to climb on the table, take her down, and say, "Tables are not for climbing. Let's go over to the climber."

Please read the section "Toddler Aggression" in the next chapter, because much may apply to this age. Children must get the consistent message that it is not okay to hurt other people.

This is the age when tantrums may begin. It is important that the child does not get her way because of a tantrum. (Of course children usually pick public places!) Just remain calm, and try to distract the child with something else as soon as the tantrum dies down.

Actually, though, the child around one year old is usually rather pleasant and sunny and fun to be around. The give and take of social relationships and play are being learned.

Social Games

Hand It Over

 With the child sitting in front of you, hand her an attractive object, and say, "Here you are." Then reach out your open hand, palm up, smile, look expectant and say, "Please give it to me." The child will probably hand it back to you. If not, gently take it back. Then say, "Thank you!" Then reach out and hold the object toward the child and repeat, "Here you are." See if you can get the child to repeat this sequence back and forth.

Hide and Seek

 Play simple versions of hide and seek. Hide yourself behind a piece of furniture with a good part of you sticking out in view. Say, "Where an I?" . . . "Here I am!" Soon the child will be able to come after you.

Catch Me

 Crawl away from the child and encourage him to come after you and catch you. Then switch roles . . . "I'm gonna get you . . ." This game is wildly exciting to children. Do be certain that you are allowing the child power . . . don't overwhelm him, but let him take the lead.

Staring

"Staring behavior" is common at this age. Sometimes an adult will be puzzled that this otherwise active child will suddenly stop and just stare at other children or activities. The child is actually taking it all in, giving mental practice before later engaging in the activity herself. They enjoy looking out the window or looking at other children playing. Sometimes simple "looking" is the most common activity other than sleeping at this age.

Physical

Climbing Stairs

Crawling up stairs, a skill that may have begun in the previous stage, now is a full-fledged compulsion. At home, there is nothing that a baby enjoys more than crawling up a flight of stairs with an adult right behind. Learning to crawl down safely is another thing. See if you can teach the child to crawl down backwards while on her tummy. Stairways need to be blocked off with gates for safety when an adult is not there to supervise this compulsion.

A small "nursery set" of stable wooden steps will find much interest from this age. The "toddler slide," a piece of equipment with a few steps, a platform with railings on both sides and a low slide is very popular. There are a number of variations.

Pulling Up

Once the child can sit up and crawl it is not long before she starts to pull up to a standing position, using any stationary object handy.

Make an effort to see that there are stable things around for a child to practice pulling up on.

Being able to stand up produces great pride of accomplishment.

Cruising

"Cruising" is the term used when children walk along side-stepping, holding on to objects such as sofas, walls or low tables.

Develop "cruising devices." See how you can arrange furniture and other stable objects to give children plenty of safe things to grab onto and walk around holding on. You might even install low railings about 18 inches off the floor. Or, perhaps a low permanent "wall" about 18 inches high can be installed in the room and serve as a room divider as well, separating the play area from the feeding, diapering and sleeping areas of the room.

Standing Alone

Once the child is good at cruising, the next step is to stand alone. Those sturdy little legs are squarely under the child in a wide stance, and balance is still wobbly. A child will usually stand alone when she is within reach of some stable object to grab onto for security. Later she will get up to a standing position from a sitting position, without the aid of something to pull up on.

Walking

The transition from cruising to walking is a gradual one. The child will walk along holding onto an adult hand, first with both hands, then with only one hand, and then with only the lightest pressure. At this point the adult hand is there mainly for security rather than support.

Then comes the milestone of the first independent step. Is there any adult who cannot react to the joy and excitement on the baby's face at this moment? It must be akin to making a first space walk in the mind of the child. Free at last!

Open spaces with soft carpeted surfaces are necessary for children learning to walk. Try to stay in control of clutter. Although there will always be toys on the floor, try to minimize the number of things to stumble over.

Climbing

This is the age of exploration. Like the mountain climber, the child will scale every large object "because it's there."

It's nice to have some safe things for children to climb on like a low climber or a large, soft chair or couch.

Dancing

Put on some lively music and children cannot stand still! In their wide stance they will rock from side to side. Or some will bend their knees and bounce up and down. Balance, coordination, and fun!

Riding Toys

Children this age also love riding on small wheeled toys. Moving across space under their own power is an exciting new experience for them. In the process of propelling these toys, they are using their feet, and gaining balance.

Towel Ride

Have the child sit on a towel on a smooth floor. Slowly pull the towel to give the child a ride across the floor. This involves balance skills and is a lot of fun for the baby.

Pushing and Pulling

Push toys and pull toys are very popular. They give children something to do with their new skill of walking, and to a certain degree motivate the child to practice the skill. (Do be assured that the child would be driven to walk without these toys.) These toys are also good because they usually make a fine noise, and let the child practice the "cause and effect" phenomenon.

Practice Moving in Different Ways

Now children have quite a repertoire of ways to move across a space. They will be kept happily occupied if a teacher focuses on giving them many interesting opportunities to use all their new skills.

Mini Obstacle Course

See if you can arrange mini "obstacle courses" for babies to crawl through, climb over, etc. Such things as fabric tunnels, sheets draped over chairs and small tables, grocery boxes, small sturdy stairs and toddler slides, pillows, round bolsters, etc. can combine to make fun places to move over, through and under.

In activities like these children are learning about their bodies in space and this has a relationship to later making sense of the placement of letters and words on a page.

Hand Coordination

At the beginning of this stage children become fascinated by and able to pick up very small objects like the tiniest piece of dust or a small bug.

First they use a "raking motion" to pick up small objects. All their fingers move together. This is, at best, an inefficient way to pick things up.

Then, they get the "pincer" muscles of thumb and forefinger to cooperate and pick up small objects.

Be conscious, especially, of removing from the environment tiny objects like staples, thumb tacks, pebbles, insects and small clumps of dirt that babies this age love to pick up and put in their mouths.

Small finger foods such as dry cereal, soft raisins, cooked peas and cooked apple chunks to pick up and eat find great interest with children this age.

Examining Objects

Provide babies with interesting objects to examine and play with. They especially like toys that "do something" when they act on them. If the toy makes a noise, if it has a moving part, if something happens, the toy will keep their attention longer.

In addition to the usual array of toys, bring in interesting household objects such as a rubber glove, a wooden spoon, a pineapple. Give children experiences with many different textures, shapes and weights of objects.

Bean Bags

Bean bags are fun for this age. Children enjoy the pure sensory feel of the bean bags. They can stack them, throw them, put them on their head and just feel them. Do check bean bags often to see that they are in good repair and the contents cannot spill out and be swallowed by children. Popcorn kernels would be good stuffing.

Exploring

The child is fascinated by cause and effect relationships . . . action A causes response B. She is learning how objects move, and about shapes and forms and textures. You can count on this little person to crawl into every space where she can fit (and try to get into some where she will not fit). She will fully examine every object, which until now she has only been able to see, and not touch. Water play fascinates. The child will put everything possible in her mouth and lick and suck on everything else.

This is the time when many babies come into direct conflict at home. It is generally advised that parents "clear the decks" as much as possible of breakable or otherwise forbidden objects. If a child hears too many "no's" at this time she may become even more rebellious in the coming toddler age, or worse, may become compliant but lose some of the natural curiosity of young children. A child's curiosity and initiative in exploring has a relationship to the development of intelligence. Most child care environments are (or should be) set up so that everything in the child's environment is available for examination. In this "yes" environment, children can investigate to their heart's content. The teacher's job is to provide interesting new things to explore from time to time, and to maintain a safe environment.

A Safe Environment

Although it was important before, it is now critical to "babyproof" the environment. Most important, stay *vigilant*. Watch children closely. Children at this age must never be unsupervised even for a moment. Here are some basic safety pointers, but don't limit yourself to these. Constantly be alert for any possibly hazardous situation.

1. Put safety plugs in all electrical outlets not in use. Extension cords are dangerous and should be used *only* for special occasions and under constant supervision.

2. Make sure no appliance cords dangle down where children can pull on them.

3. Put safety latches on low cabinet doors and drawers.

4. Keep diaper pails covered, and in a place that's inaccessible to babies.

5. Make sure toys are in good repair and there are no sharp edges.

6. Make sure the environment is free of small objects children can choke on. Objects should be at least the size of a child's fist to be considered safe. Watch especially for toys of older children that may have small pieces dangerous to babies.

7. Make sure there are no small sharp objects around that could cause damage if swallowed: safety pins, staples, thumb tacks, paper clips, hair pins, chipped paint, nails, etc.

8. Loose carpet could cause beginning walkers to trip and fall.

9. Use furniture with rounded edges.

10. Make sure wooden furniture and toys are free of splinters.

11. Buy furniture with maximum stability.

12. Do not leave purses within sight or reach of babies. They are irresistible, and often contain potentially dangerous things.

13. Store all medicine, including adult aspirin and pills that may be in purses, in a place totally inaccessible to children. Always keep them in the original container, with child proof tops.

14. Store all cleaning materials and poisonous substances in places inaccessible to children. Purchase supplies with child proof tops.

15. Do not drink coffee or other hot beverages around babies. A single cup of coffee spilled on a child can cause a third degree scald burn over 80% of the child's body.

16. Inspect water temperature from hot water faucets and adjust down if necessary. Water should not be warmer than 110 degrees.

17. Doors can be very dangerous. Put signs on the outside of doors warning people to open slowly and carefully, in case a child is behind it. Fingers caught in doors are a frequent injury of young children. Try to discourage children from playing near doors. Be careful when opening and closing doors.

18. Tie cords from blinds or draperies high, and out of reach of children.

19. Never leave a child unattended on the changing table.

20. Check to make sure that any plants in the room are non-poisonous, and keep out of reach of children.

21. Keep cages of any classroom pets clean and the area around them free of debris.

22. Make sure there are no gaps in fences and gates of outdoor play areas.

23. Keep sharp objects like scissors and knives out of reach.

24. Check your outdoor area for any potential hazards—berries, debris that may have blown in, animal feces, etc.

The most obvious safety factor again, is a supervisor of children who is thinking and watchful.

Language

Children show that they understand their first words in this stage. They often don't *produce* words until much later.

Among the first words a child typically learns are "mommy,"
"daddy," "bye-bye," and "baby."

"Where's . . . "

*Try asking, "Where's Mommy?" while you are hold-
ing the child and her mother is close by and there are
several other people in the room to choose from. If she
turns to her mother and smiles, you have an indication
that she knows what that particular combination of
sounds means. Try this with other familiar people.*

Action Commands

*Try giving children simple commands such as "Wave
bye-bye," "Give me a hug," "Sit down," and "Come here."
Of course, you will express pleasure when the child com-
plies.*

Again, be conscious of your role as a language model. Talk
constantly about what's happening in front of the child's eyes.
Name objects as you hand them to children.

Jargon Continues

This non-verbal child is by no means silent! The string of
often funny sounding babbling sounds goes on and on. Occasionally you will hear an almost recognizable word slip in. It is as
though the child is "pretending" to talk. It's probably mostly the
sensory enjoyment of having sounds come out of his mouth.
(Hmmm . . . know any adults like that?)

Call and Response

*Sometimes you can catch a child calling out a string
of nonsense syllables: "Da-da-da!" Call the very same
sequence of syllables back. Give the child a chance to call
them back to you again. See if you can get it going back
and forth several times. Conversation!*

Books

It's not too early to give children books to look at. Although you will want to keep certain books "special" and only show them to children when they are on your lap and you can insure gentle handling, children should have books they can carry around and handle themselves. Sturdy "toddler" board books or some of the homemade books described below give children pictures to look at and later name. The beauty of homemade books is that you can tailor them to the vocabulary and interest of particular children. Start now to build in an addiction to books.

Zip Closure Bag Books

Sew together 4 or 5 sandwich size plastic bags with zip closures along the bottom edge. A simple whip stitch works well. Cut pieces of light cardboard to just fit inside the bags. This will stiffen the pages and make them easier to turn, while providing a background for pictures you insert. Cut pictures from magazines and slip them on both sides of the cardboard in the bags.

Contact-Paper Homemade Book

1. Make a simple book by laying several pieces of paper on top of each other and folding them in half. Staple in the fold.

2. Now draw or glue pictures on each page.

3. Unroll some transparent contact paper, peel off the backing, and place it on a table sticky side up. Open the book and place it on the contact paper so that two side by side pages are covered at once. Press down and smooth out any bubbles. Cut off the contact paper close to the edges. Do this to all double pages of the book.

This is an excellent way to add life to purchased paper bound books as well.

Photo Album Book

Spiral-bound photo albums with magnetic plastic film over cardboard pages make excellent homemade books for toddlers. Photos or magazine pictures placed in the pages can be changed from time to time to keep interest high. The stiff sturdy pages are easy for toddlers to turn.

Focus

1. Children this age need the opportunity to practice new physical skills. They need space in a safe, open environment to do this.

2. They should be offered many interesting objects to examine and explore to feed their developing curiosity.

3. In order to venture out into the wide world of discovery, they need a feeling of comfort and security with their caregiver. The caregiver must express pleasure and pride in the child's new accomplishments and encourage an eager "greet the world" attitude.

CHAPTER 4

The Toddler

There is probably no "cuter" stage of child, and no more difficult stage to be with all day long than the toddler between about 15 months and two years of age. The toddler is totally lovable and engaging, curious and "into everything," egocentric, demanding, extreme in moods, and high in energy. It may be very tiring and even exasperating at times dealing with toddlers day in and day out. But it's such a fascinating age! So much progress is made in such a short time. Toddlers are in the act of discovering the world. Now that they can walk, the world is theirs to possess!

This age group requires a teacher with great energy, flexibility, patience, nurturing ability, and vigilance!

Please check back to the previous chapter's section about "child-proofing" the environment. This "toddler" child is every bit as capable and more so of getting himself into serious trouble exploring the environment.

Social-Emotional

"Egocentricity." That's the word that most aptly describes children this age in relationship to other people. In the mind of the toddler the whole world exists only for his pleasure and service. Some toddlers even seem to become rather "aloof," in contrast to the engaging, flirtatious children they were just a few months earlier.

Children engage mostly in "solitary play" at this age. Of course, there are exceptions, but most often the child is in his own little world and largely ignores other children. Where two year olds enjoy playing near other children, younger toddlers could care less. Of course, it's pretty hard to ignore a room full of other children! Toddlers in group care tend to be more advanced in social awareness of other children.

Developing Empathy

Often young toddlers will treat other children like objects or toys put there for their examination and poke eyes, pull hair, etc. These gestures may not be meant to hurt the other child . . . the toddler doesn't really realize that other people can "hurt." Rather, they do these things to "explore" what the other "child-object" is good for . . . interesting noises, etc.

The caregiver has an important role here. First of all, you must protect the children from each other! Part of the vigilance we talked about was not only keeping your room free of safety hazards but also keeping a close eye on the children themselves. That is one of several reasons state licensing regulations require low staff/child ratios with this age group.

Secondly, this is the time to start teaching children about kindness and empathy. Actually, there can be surprising touches of empathy in toddlers. If a child in the room hurts himself or cries, another toddler may come over and try to comfort him. He may offer a toy or his blanket. This is the way a toddler would also try to comfort his tired daddy . . . with something the toddler would be comforted with himself. (Egocentricity.) This behavior is not consistent. The same toddler may comfort a child once, and ignore distress another time, depending upon his mood. Children learn about empathy by seeing it modeled by adults. If *you* and other important adults in the child's life show concern and solicitous kindness when a child is hurt, children will learn from you.

Toddler Aggression

When a toddler hurts another child it is important to react

with clarity. Come over quickly. Comfort the victim, and state very strongly to the aggressor child that it is not OK to hurt people. If the child has scratched another child, for instance, bring the child face to face with the victim. Show the marks. Say, "Look! You hurt Joey! Look at his eyes . . . he's crying because it hurts. It's not OK to hurt people. I don't want you to scratch anymore." Don't worry if you think the child will not understand all your words. Your facial expression and tone of voice will communicate your meaning. Be serious and stern without yelling. When you yell, the child becomes frightened and all other messages are lost. It may help to have the aggressor go with you to get a cloth to wash off the scratch. He should see you comforting the victim. This advice goes for all kinds of hurting — hitting, biting, scratching, hair pulling, pushing, poking, etc.

Some theoretical textbooks will tell you to ignore negative behaviors so they will go away. Don't pay attention to this advice with toddlers, and older preschool children, for that matter, when it comes to hurting others. If you ignore aggression, young children will think you approve of it. Even other children in the room will think you approve if you do not react to the aggressor.

Some teachers report success with giving the aggressor a brief "time-out" away from other children, meaning usually sitting down at the side of the room. Although this works with older children, it is a bit more difficult with toddlers. They are unlikely to stay put very long if you move them to a different spot in the room. You might say, "You sit here a few minutes until you can play without hurting other people." Try to ignore him and go on with the other routines of the class. Then, in two or three minutes, the slate wiped clean, involve the child in something totally different from what he was doing before.

Do not react to a child's aggression against other children by physically punishing the child. Remember, a toddler's main method of learning social behaviors is imitating the important adults in his life. If you slap or spank a child, he will become more aggressive. If you show the child how to react with kindness, he will learn kindness. Unfortunately, this does not happen overnight. You must remain vigilant and consistent.

Sometimes a toddler program will have a child who hurts other children a lot. Often his parents are as distressed about it as you are. While toddlers are very demanding, they can become frustrated very quickly. They don't have words to get what they want or even express their frustration, so they take action physically. The first, and admittedly simplistic advice is to watch that child like a hawk. If you see frustration building step in quickly. Try to teach the child to use words . . . although with some toddlers this is a long way off. When a child this age acts with great aggression, it does not mean he is destined to carry a switch blade. It is very likely a "stage" in the truest sense of the word. After many efforts you and the parents may decide that the child is not best served in group care at this time in his life. By all means, invite the parents to try the program in another six months. Things may go much better at that time.

Independence

This is the age of the drive for "autonomy." "Me do it byself!!!" The child is in a constant drive to establish himself as a separate individual. Therefore he pushes away from his mother and caregiver, and resists suggestions. "No" is one of the first words. Loud protests are common. The confusing thing is that this same contrary, independent person is often suddenly clinging, climbing on laps, asking for help, and generally very cuddly and cozy. Back and forth. The child frequently needs to go back to "home base," the trusted adult, to reestablish a feeling of security before again venturing out.

The children are not as cuddly as they were a few months ago. They will be hugged and "loved" on their own terms only. Too busy.

In dealing with a toddler's independence and "contrariness" it's best to avoid a showdown. Instead of telling a child to do something, or asking if he would like to (a sure way to get a "no" response), offer two "yes" choices. "Would you like apples or oranges for snack?"

Develop a consistent daily routine, doing things in the same order every day. If you have your story time every day after snack, children will often go to your story corner without being told.

Leave the bulk of your day fairly loose and unstructured, allowing children to play where they choose. If you bring out a special toy or activity it will attract children without a lot of directives from you.

Sharing

Don't expect toddlers to share naturally. We must again go back to their egocentricity. They simply cannot put themselves in another person's shoes. Yet there is much adults can do to guide the child in this direction.

Consciously model sharing behavior yourself, and talk about it. "I brought some graham crackers and I'm going to share them with all of you." "Come over here, Sheila. I will share my playdough with you." They have to know what the word "share" means before they can learn to do it. Later you can ask, "Sheldon, will you share you playdough with me? Thank you! That makes me happy." Next, judging the mood and likelihood for success, you can ask a child, "Jennifer, will you share your playdough with Seth? He doesn't have any." Express appreciation if there is compliance. "I bet Seth is happy." By all means, if you notice rare spontaneous sharing, draw subtle attention to it. "Tamara felt happy when you let her have the truck."

Tantrums

Again, because children at this age have few words to express frustration, and very little actual power, they often resort to tantrums. It may not be a conscious ploy to get one's way. (That comes later.) Toddlers are people of extremes. A polite protest is not within their range of social responses. Even the slightest annoyance may lead to kicking and screaming. Treat the tantrum with patience ... don't match it ... and patiently let the child see that it will not help her get her way.

One fortunate, if not totally consistent thing is, that toddlers are generally more cooperative with babysitters and caregivers than they are with their own parents. They're sure mommy loves them ... but not so sure and willing to take chances with the rest of the world. Maintain your sense of humor, and "stay light."

Short Attention Span

One difficulty in dealing with a group of toddlers is their extremely short attention span. They are very distractable. "A lick and a promise" is all they give most activities. The world is just too exciting to spend much time doing just one thing.

Their very distractability can work to your advantage when the child is being difficult. If the child is vehemently demanding a certain object, for instance, he can be quite easily distracted with another interesting object.

There are a few techniques that help keep the attention of toddlers for a few minutes longer.

1. The "flop down and do" technique. Instead of calling toddlers over and trying to get them all to sit down and pay attention at the same time, simply flop down on the floor and start doing whatever it was you wanted to present to them. At first two or three children will see you and come over. Then more children will want to get in on the action. They stay longer when it was their choice to come over in the first place.

2. Entice children over with a novelty factor. Bring out something different that they haven't seen that day. A music box they haven't heard will stop everyone dead in their tracks! See the "Surprise Bag" activity described in the next chapter. This works like magic with toddlers as well.

3. Do simple art projects with only a few children at a time. Set up the activity for one child, and have paper and crayons available for a few "watchers" while they wait their turn. (Have other activities the "watchers" could be doing elsewhere in the room if they wish. They should be there by free choice.) Whether it is finger painting, painting with a brush, dribbling and smearing colored glue, or scribbling, the artist won't take long. The watchers are gaining mental practice.

4. One on one, the attention of toddlers is increased. A child who has the undivided attention of one adult will be able to sustain interest in an activity much longer. Find the child who cannot listen to a story at group time. Put him on your lap in the corner with the same book, just the two of you, and he'll probably stay with you longer.

Conservatism

Toddlers are conservatives. They don't like change. They like to feel comfortable in knowing what is going to happen next. You can eliminate a lot of problems by having a good, solid basic routine. Your routine can be augmented by "rituals." Rituals are little things that are done day in and day out in exactly the same way. They can be a way of saying, "All's right with the world." Your puppet comes out first thing every morning when you all sit down and says good morning to everyone. You put on the same record of march music every day at clean-up time. You say the same poem each day before lunch. You tuck in each child individually and sing the same lullaby at nap time. When children get comfortable with rituals it will be easier to teach them such things as washing hands after going to the bathroom, and hanging up their coat when they come inside.

Fantasy Play

It is in the toddler year that the child first starts to engage in fantasy play, or "pretend play." It was only a short time ago that he demonstrated his first ability at "abstract thinking" learning about "object permanence" — that something continues to exist even when one cannot see it. Fantasy play involves having a mental image of an object . . . and then "projecting" that mental image onto some other object.

This starts in the toddler year when the child uses one object to represent something else. It is usually confined to objects. We frequently see it first with a child using a toy telephone. Children will also mimic other adult behaviors they have seen often. They will carry a purse over their arm, stir a pot with a wooden spoon, wash dishes in a tub of soapy water, and tenderly cover a doll with a small blanket.

Toddlers may also pretend to be something else. Often one will see "kitties" or "doggies" crawling around on the toddler room floor. This is one instance when children will imitate each other. It is always surprising to hear "motorcycle noises" coming out of toddlers . . . usually learned from playing with older siblings.

This fantasy play is a significant mental development. Children are using their minds in different, more flexible ways. Learning to imagine . . . the first step in stretching the human potential.

Physical

Once the child learns to walk, the next step is to run! There is the insatiable drive to explore every space and climb everything climbable. There are plenty of stumbles and falls as the child develops competency on his feet. "Gross motor activity," using large muscles of arms, legs and trunk, is clearly the most dominant drive of toddlers. Their energy is incredible. They spend a lot of time just wandering. Their attention span is so short that their wandering may seem almost aimless as they move from one object to another in the room.

Toddlers "toddle." They stand and walk with feet wide apart and arms out from the side or bent upward for balance. Their belly-button is the first thing to meet the world as they walk around with stomachs protruding. They often walk while holding onto objects in each hand, as though for security.

It doesn't take long for toddlers to gain skill at getting up and down from the floor quickly, and "squatting." They enjoy bending over and looking at the world from between their legs.

They hate being confined — in a playpen, car seat, crib or highchair. This is the age when they will learn to climb out of almost anything and free themselves from constraints like an escape artist . . . and as a result experience sometimes serious falls. In a child care center for safety reasons as well as accommodating the child's growing autonomy, this is a good time to start seating children on small chairs at low tables for meals, instead of in highchairs, and sleeping on cots or mats rather than in cribs.

It is highly advisable to have a stable, "toddler sized" climbing apparatus in the room for toddlers. That will make it easier to "redirect" them from climbing on chairs, tables, and shelves.

Balls of all kinds are great for toddlers. Inflatable beach balls are especially good because they are big and the child feels powerful being able to pick up something so large. Although toddlers are not good at kicking a ball because it is too difficult to balance on one foot while swinging the other, they sort of "run into" balls or shove them to make them move.

Throwing

Toddler Basket Ball

Toddlers enjoy throwing things but have minimal skill hitting a target. The teacher can hold out a large plastic laundry basket and catch balls thrown by toddlers in her general direction from three or four feet away.

Soft Ball

Toddlers' compulsion for throwing can be safely met indoors or outdoors with this simple to make "ball." Simply stuff polyester fiberfill stuffing into a double layer of nylon stocking and knot at both ends. "Support hose" last a little longer. These will not hurt people or objects when thrown. They can also be thrown into the washer and dryer.

Stacking

Stacking things up and knocking them down again is lots of fun. Cardboard blocks are popular in toddler programs because they are light and manageable by toddlers.

Diaper Box Blocks

Let toddlers help you wad up newspaper and stuff disposable diaper boxes. Then tape the boxes shut. Now you have very large, light-weight blocks that toddlers love to lift and stack. They feel very powerful being able to lift something big.

Moving

Empty cardboard grocery boxes provide endless entertainment. Children will climb in and out of them, turn them on their side, sit on them, and push them around the room, giving dolls a ride.

They enjoy "dancing" to record player music, rocking from side to side in their wide toddler stance, or wiggling their behinds.

Follow the leader games with the teacher leading find great success with toddlers. They will enjoy imitating almost any movement you can think up.

An outside play area with grass, shade, a space for running and something interesting to climb on, as well as sand for digging adds greatly to your program.

Riding toys, pull toys and push toys that make a noise appeal to toddlers and they can use them on the move.

Hand Coordination

They enjoy handling objects. As well as putting things in their mouths, they will examine an object from all sides, then try to figure out all the different things one can do with it.

Rotating their wrists to manipulate objects is a new, not well-developed skill. This is an important skill in learning to put puzzles together. Wooden inlay puzzles with single shapes are good for toddler programs. Some come with large knobs, making it easy for toddlers to grasp pieces. It is sometimes surprising and frustrating for an observing adult to see how hard it can be for the toddler to get the shape into place.

Toddlers are especially fascinated by sticking things through holes. The traditional "shape boxes" are challenging and difficult for them. First they have to perceive the shape of the hole and the shape of the piece. When that is accomplished (often not until late in the toddler year) the child must hold the piece and rotate his wrist just right, as with puzzles, to make the piece fit. Often he will just try to jam it through the hole.

A good way to make a less frustrating "beginner's shape box" is simply to cut a hole in a coffee can lid. The child will enjoy sticking all manner of small objects through this hole.

Likewise, boxes with slots in them are fun. Toddlers will enjoy putting pieces of junk mail through a slot in a cardboard "mailbox."

Screwing on jar lids is a new and challenging skill that also involves rotating the wrist. See if you can find a plastic jar with a lid about 2 inches in diameter that the child can grasp easily. The child will also enjoy sticking his hand inside the jar to grasp objects.

Toys with pieces to fit together are interesting to toddlers. Nesting and stacking toys are also just right. Plastic bowls of the same size make the easiest nesting toys, because they will fit together in any order. They will interest young toddlers because they look so different when they are nested together than when they are separate and spread out in front of the toddlers.

Emptying and filling things becomes a passion with toddlers . . . and yes, they do more emptying than filling! Light plastic shovels and sand pails, or margarine tubs and scoops from coffee cans will get much eager use in a sandbox. In the process of filling up a pail with sand they are gaining experience making the hand do what the mind wants it to do.

Dumping can be refined to pouring. Playing with water is a compulsion with toddlers. A dishpan of water with a few plastic cups, spray can tops, a small pitcher, coffee scoops, etc. will get concentrated attention from toddlers.

Many "art" projects give toddlers a chance to practice their

fine motor skills: playdough (the all-time toddler favorite), finger
painting, brush painting, pasting, scribbling, etc. They can grasp
a fat crayon using a clumsy full fist hold and enjoy scribbling.

Sensory Activities

Toddlers will enjoy activities that use all the senses. Think
about how you can add a "sensory dimension" as you plan.
Playdough, water play, sand, smelling activities, music boxes, all
can be used in many ways that will interest toddlers. Remember,
of course, that taste seems to be the dominant sense at this age.
Absolutely everything goes in the mouth, so be very conscious of
safety and hygiene.

Music Box Hide and Seek

*While children are not looking, wind up a music
box, and hide it somewhere in the room where children
can find it. Can they follow the sound to locate the music
box?*

Cause and Effect

Experiments in "causality" fascinate toddlers. "Action A produces response B." They are in the age of exploration, not only in
exploring every physical space, but in exploring every property
of every object they come across. As these little Einsteins cover
the earth, nothing is safe from their experiments and investigations.

Toilet Training

Although some parents think about starting toilet training
during the toddler year, and some children are successful, most
children are over two before they are successful. Please refer to
the discussion of this topic in the chapter on two year olds.

The time and attention demands of changing diapers and
beginning toilet training, and generally managing the "hygiene"
of group care for toddlers is another reason for low staff/child
ratios in group child care situations for toddlers. Proper handwashing procedures and general cleaning of surfaces in the toddler environment is of critical importance in protecting the

health of children. The Center for Disease Control in Atlanta, GA has developed a set of training materials for child care staff on this topic. They describe simple procedures that will substantially cut down on the incidence of illness in child care centers. These materials are available from your state health department anywhere in the country. No child care center should be without them.

Language

It's getting interesting now. The "jargon" or random babbling and stringing together of nonsense syllables of earlier stages continues. This babbling is really an "alphabet soup" as children practice all the sounds, intonations and rhythms of their native language. Although toddlers vary greatly in their production of speech, most are coming out with their first words at this time. There will be an exciting span of time when a child seems to be saying new words almost every day. Also you will be aware that children are understanding more and more of what you say to them.

Children usually start by naming familiar objects and saying common social phrases: "Mama," "Doggie," "Spoon," "Bye-bye!" "Hi!" "Night night," "Mine!" "Thank you!" Soon two word phrases emerge: "My ball," "Mo juice!"

The Envelope of Language

The best way for caregivers to enhance language development in children is to provide a good "envelope of language," surrounding the child with meaningful talk.

Just having a lot of language around children is not sufficient. "Canned language" from a radio or TV doesn't count. The talk must be from a live human being, and it must be about the "here and now." Two adults talking about what they did yesterday will have little meaning for the toddler. But if you talk about what the child sees going on in front of him, understanding of language will be enriched.

Talk to yourself as you go about the routines of the day. Describe what you are doing. "I'm washing my hands now to get this green paint off my fingers." "I am putting the spaghetti on

your plate now." And talk about what the children are doing.
"Oh . . . Teddy fell down." "You are rocking back and forth, back
and forth in the rocking chair." "Here comes Jessie, riding on the
horsie." This provides the "sensory connection" that will allow
the child to associate things and actions with the sounds (words)
that represent them.

Expand on the child's words. The child says, "Ball!" You say,
"Oh, do you want to play with the ball? I'll get it for you." This
gives children the model for putting together longer phrases and
sentences themselves eventually. They are absorbing language
rules of syntax and sentence structure. These more complex sentences won't show up in children's speech for at least another
year or so, but you are at the "data input" stage.

New Words Emphasis

*When a child first comes out with a new word, write
it on a chalkboard or bulletin board in the room so that
other staff and parents at home can emphasize it and
use it many times.*

Words of the Week

*Some teachers like to identify several words each
week which they will emphasize. They make parents
aware of them and involve them in activities all week.*

Of course, pronunciation is often way off. Don't worry about
it or make any attempt to correct pronunciation at this stage. Do
speak clearly yourself, though. "Baby talk" was fine for its social
aspects in the first year of the child's life. Now it's best to model
the correct pronunciation of words. This is the time when families
develop fun, "pet words" generated from toddlers that stay
around forever and become family tradition. This is no big problem. In the child care center, though, you represent the wider
world . . . best to stick to traditional language.

Keep in mind the difference between "receptive language"
and "productive language." Receptive language is what the child
hears and understands. Productive language is words and
phrases the child manages to say. There is often, at this stage
particularly, a wide gap between the two. A child between one

and two years of age understands many more words than he is able to produce in his own speech. Parents should not worry if the child is producing very few words, as long as he demonstrates that he understands things. Ask him to get you some things. "Teddy, bring me the book on the table." "Close the door." "Where's the doggie?"

Comprehension Games

Body Parts

Play the "touch your nose" game, asking the child to touch various body parts, or point to people or objects in the room. "Show me your ears." "Where's your foot?" "Where's Judy?"

Toddlers genuinely enjoy pointing to pictures on a page in a book. "Where's the elephant?"

"Whazzat"

Later toddlers will enjoy pointing to objects or pictures of objects and naming them. "Airplane!" Sometimes they play a "whazzat?" game. They point to something and ask, "Whazzat?" and you supply the word. Then they repeat the word.

Child: (pointing) "Whazzat?"

You: "That's an apple."

Child: "Apo."

You: "That's right. That's an apple."

Picture Thing Match

Make drawings or take photographs of several familiar things in the room. Show the child the picture, and play the "Whazzat?" game. Then see if the child can take the picture over to the real object in the room.

Pack a Bag

You or a puppet could produce a small suitcase. Tell the child to go and get one object at a time to put in the

suitcase. "Get me a blanket to put in my suitcase."
"Thank you!" "Now get me a book . . ."

Books

As stated in the previous chapter, this is a good time to get children addicted to books.

Good books for toddlers have very clear, realistic, uncomplicated illustrations or photographs. Picture books with one thing on each page are good. Children also enjoy books that have an unusual shape, or are interesting to feel with various textures inside.

Since toddlers are very rough on books, you will want to keep some books on a high shelf and only bring them out to read to children at special times. However, toddlers should also have the experience and pleasure of handling books and turning the pages themselves. Here is where you can use some of the sturdy home-made alternatives described in the previous chapter.

Nursery Rhymes

The old Mother Goose rhymes and the simple melodies that go with them are just right for this age. It doesn't matter that they don't understand every single word. Who does? It's the bouncy rhythms and funny sounds that are appealing. You are reinforcing the idea that language is fun to play with. Toddlers will not be able to actually recite the rhymes, but they may join in on particular phrases occasionally.

A nicely illustrated book of nursery rhymes and simple poetry is a good addition to your book collection at this time. The pictures will enhance the enjoyment of the sounds.

Music

Music and language production are closely related in the early years. If you sing a lot, your children will sing a lot. They will not, except in very rare cases, be able to hold a tune. Young toddlers won't even sing a song along with you . . . but their voices will "fade in and out" of your songs. Every now and then you may notice them chanting particular words or phrases as they engage in solitary play. It is not uncommon to hear a little voice sing out, "Ee-ei-ee-ei-o."

An easy book for the "non-musical teacher" is *Piggyback Songs for Infants and Toddlers* by Jean Warren, Warren Publishing, Inc.

When you sing a lot, you are modelling another way to use your voice to express yourself. A room that has singing in it is usually a happy room.

Music can help to set the tone of your classroom. While not advocating a "musak" approach with constant background music, at certain times of day music on the record player can make things go more smoothly. Happy, peppy music on the record player in the morning can make a child care center seem less empty and more cheerful. Soft classical music can calm children down before nap time.

Lullabies

There is nothing nicer than having someone sing you your own personal lullaby. (Can you remember?) At nap time when children are drifting off to sleep, a gentle touch on the head or a back rub accompanied by the singing voice of a favorite grown-up gives children a sense of security that allows them to relax and drift off.

Likewise, rocking and singing to a child who is crying and upset, perhaps because mommy just left, will often calm the child better than any words you can produce. Whereas toddlers don't always understand the meaning of words, music communicates. Fred Rogers' simple song, "I'm Taking Care of You" (*Mr. Rogers' Songbook*, Random House, 1970), is one of my favorites for this.

What Is Pre-Reading For Toddlers?

1. Vocabulary development. Learning about talk. Before children can interpret "talk written down," they must have a basic facility with language. The toddler year is when children start to understand and use words. Focus on introducing a wide range of words in a meaningful context.

2. Adults loving books. If the child sees important adults enjoying books for their own pleasure, this is likely to be imitated.

3. Looking at pictures. Being able to "read" pictures and see that they represent something else that is real is an early pre-reading skill.

4. Adult reading picture books to children. The child associates reading with pleasant social interaction with favorite adults.

5. Handling books. Toddlers should have their own books to handle and love.

Focus

1. Accommodating the child's growing drive for autonomy must be balanced with a secure routine and clear and reasonable limits. The daily plan should allow many opportunities for toddlers to make free choices with the security of a caring adult nearby.

2. Toddlers need to be able to explore a safe environment and be active, developing all their new gross motor skills. The teacher should plan an environment that is varied and interesting in the challenges it presents.

3. Simple activities and materials that involve "cause and effect" relationships fascinate toddlers and give them practice in problem solving and reasoning.

4. The ability to understand language is growing rapidly this year. The teacher should build in many rich language experiences into the daily routine and activities planned.

CHAPTER 5

The Two Year Old

So much is happening this year. The most exciting area is language development and the blossoming of speech. Another interesting development is the beginning of pretend play—playing with dolls, dishes and dress up clothes. The child is slowly becoming more aware of others and their feelings. Successful toilet training often happens in this year. There is often a change in behavior of the generally cooperative two year old when two and a half comes around, which may be a more turbulent time.

The teacher of two year olds needs to be nurturing, warm, understanding, flexible, very alert, and devoted to two year olds! She or he must not mind changing diapers.

Social-Emotional

You've heard about the "terrible twos." Well, most teachers of two year olds tell me they're not so terrible. It's just a matter of making your expectations match the capabilities of the age.

Stubbornness

Like toddlers, two year olds are still working through the "autonomy" business, establishing their independent identity.

They can be contrary and stubborn. But sometimes they are better behaved in a child care situation than they are at home. They enjoy other children so much that they are generally cooperative with a teacher.

Two and a half can be a more difficult age than early two, although children differ when they reach this difficult stage, and how long they stay in it.

Try to figure out ways to give children "power" in your room. Let them move chairs around. Let them decide where to hang their paintings and give them the tape to do it themselves. Let them help decide what to do that day. "Shall I put puzzles or playdough on that table?" Let them "win" sometimes. If a child won't come over to listen to a story, don't make a "big deal" out of it. "Entice" children into activities, rather than directing them.

Adjustment Difficulties

Adjusting to a new child care setting can still be quite difficult for this age, partly because of their stubbornness, and partly because children are very strongly attached to their mothers. As with younger children, you need to let the child develop trust in you. Do not tell the child to stop crying and be a big girl. Accept her sadness. Words can help at this age. "Sarah is sad. She is crying because she misses her mommy." You are very likely to get empathetic responses from other children. "How can we make Sarah feel better?" Comfort and reassure the child. "Mommy is coming back this afternoon after we have our snack. I am going to take good care of you, because I like you a lot." The two year old loves parallel play, so try to involve her in something other children are doing. Playdough or water play are often good ice breakers.

Short Attention Span

Although the attention span of two year olds is certainly short, it is considerably longer than that of toddlers. Keep your success ratio high by cutting off your group activities before their attention ends, and entice them with activities that involve several senses. Puppets are more interesting to listen to than teachers. A story is more fun with the aid of a flannel board.

Typical Problems

Hitting, grabbing toys away from other children, screaming, tantrums, stubbornness and refusing are the behavior problems most often listed by teachers of two year olds.

Please take a look at the discussion of toddler aggression in the previous chapter. It applies equally to two year olds.

The development of language skills has a tremendous influence on children's ability to handle frustration. Work hard to give children words to handle their anger, and help interpret children to each other. "Shawna, do you hear Maria? She is saying 'Mine!' She is playing with that right now. Let's find another one for you." "Angelo, ask Frankie, 'Can I play with that too?'" Get in there and help negotiate. You can really make a lot of progress with children in this year in getting them to express their needs.

Parallel Play

Toddlers were mostly involved in "solitary play" — everyone doing his own thing, and not paying much attention to what anybody else was doing. Two year olds, however, are developing a great interest in other children.

Socially, two year olds are "groupies." They really enjoy being near other children. They will often imitate what other children are doing. One child will sit in the sandbox and bang his shovel on the sand and say, "Bang, bang, bang!" A child next to him will look at him and smile, and bang his shovel three times and say, "Bang, bang, bang!" One girl will run across the room yelling and dive into a pile of pillows. Other children will join her in the identical activity. Although there is not much give and take, they are taking their cues from each other.

This is one reason why simple group activities like looking at a flannel board story or moving together in similar ways to creative movement records can find success with two year olds. "Come over here with us and do what we're doing," is an invitation that may be hard to refuse for a two year old.

Chair Train

Two year olds seem to love pushing all the chairs in

the room together to make a long "train," and then sitting on the chairs and making train noises. This is a good match for the age because it's parallel play — they're all doing the same thing, near each other, and they feel powerful moving furniture around.

Fantasy Play

The beginnings of fantasy play were seen in the toddler year when children used objects to represent something else. Two year olds add their ability for parallel play to their fantasy play. They enjoy being in the same place doing the same thing with other children. When children are together in the housekeeping corner, there is not a lot of dialogue and give and take. You are more likely to have three "mommies" taking care of babies than children with family roles assigned.

They enjoy putting on hats, carrying around purses, setting a table and pretending to cook and care for a baby, all things they have seen many times over. If you have doll highchairs and doll beds, make sure they are large enough and sturdy enough for a child to fit in . . . because they will surely try. Make sure you do not start "sex-role stereotyping" at this early age. Make boys as well as girls welcome in the housekeeping corner. Find "props" that are as realistic as possible. The more things look like the real thing, the more they will be used.

Most of the pretend play of two year olds will center around family roles . . . something with which they are very familiar.

Physical

The stiff gait of the toddler is smoothing out. The child bends knees and ankles more when walking, swinging arms at her side.

In fact, the two year old is enjoying a wide variety of movements. Teachers can concentrate on finding activities that allow children to practice moving in many different ways. Two year olds can jump, hop, roll and climb well.

Climbing

It is still a good idea to have a climber in the classroom. It will be much used and greatly enjoyed by children. A climber with a slide and a tunnel and several spaces to explore is lots of fun for this age. There are a number of good ones on the market.

An outdoor climber will be eagerly explored. This does take close adult supervision. Occasionally a child will get "stuck" up high and afraid to climb down. Instead of immediately lifting her down, try to tell the child where to put her hands and feet so she can make it down herself.

Creative Movement

Two year olds really enjoy creative movement games and records, exploring all the different ways they can make their bodies move. Many of these activities also involve dramatic play . . . pretending to be something else.

A simple follow the leader game will get eager participation. Simply hop, jump, tip toe and crawl around the room and you will find children behind you doing the same thing. Outside, suggest simple things like: "Let's pretend to be birds!" and "fly" around the playground. If you are fortunate enough to have a slight incline in the yard, children will love rolling down it. Rolling provides good torso muscle exercise.

Balloon Tennis

Open out a wire coat hanger into a square, as illustrated. Stretch a nylon stocking over it and tape it to the

*handle. Straighten the handle out and cover thickly with
tape so that there are no sharp pointed ends.*

*Blow up some balloons and tie them off. Children
throw the balloons up in the air and try to keep them in
the air by batting them with the coat hanger rackets.*

*This activity provides good exercise for torso muscles
and is good for developing balance. Two year olds have
remarkable success at it because the balloons float down
slowly. Children feel powerful.*

*It is possible to play this game inside. It is ideal for
providing some active movement on rainy days.*

*Put away balloons when you are through playing
the game and do not allow broken balloons to lie around.
Children have choked on balloon rubber.*

Riding Toys

Riding toys are wildly popular. Toward the end of the year a
two year old may be able to master a tricycle, with great feelings
of pride and power. Children not only benefit from the exercise
provided by riding toys, but also from the dramatic play potential, as they become motorcycles, trucks and cars. Can you make
a "track" or "road" for children to follow on riding toys?

Hand Coordination

Hand muscles are cooperating with the brain more and
more, with practice.

Simple wooden inlay puzzles, large beads to string, fit-
together toys, large pegs and pegboards, give practice for fine
motor control, and are enjoyed by this age.

Eye-droppers

*Let children transfer colored water from one small
container to another using an eye-dropper. They will be
gaining skill making their thumb and forefinger work
together. Dropping colored water onto white paper towels
makes pretty designs.*

Meat Basters

The "mega" version of the above, meat basters allow children to use the muscles of their whole hand together. Since meat basters in the water table are sometimes used to squirt other children, you might want to set this up as an individual activity, giving the child two small buckets, or a dog dish, and invite them to transfer the water from one container to the other using the baster.

Meat Tray Inlay Puzzles

To increase the number of puzzles you have available to children, cut simple shapes out of styrofoam meat trays to make puzzles. You can make these very simple by just having one shape cut out, or more complex by having small, medium or large versions of the same shape, or several different shapes.

Cutting

It is still very difficult for the child to manipulate scissors with success.

Cutting Playdough

Show children how to roll out "snakes" of playdough. Then using rounded tip scissors, they will enjoy snipping off sections of the snake. This is easy, and it gives practice using the muscles of the hand necessary for cutting. Make sure children are holding scissors correctly when they do this so they are exercising the right muscles. When the "snake" is all cut up, they can squeeze it all together again and roll out a new snake.

In the process they are getting some practice with another concept, "conservation of matter." That is the idea that the amount of a substance remains the same when it is separated into little pieces. They really won't catch on to this idea for a couple of years yet.

Tongs Transfer

Let children use kitchen tongs to transfer small toys from one container to another.

Self-Help Skills

The child can feed herself with reasonable success. Staff should not be feeding two year olds. Don't be fussy about manners. Do sit at the table and eat with the children so you can provide a *model* for good manners.

A two year old can pull on clothing, although buttoning and snapping are difficult, and tying shoes is a long way off. Especially at this toilet training period, encourage parents to dress children in clothing the child can handle independently. Let the child do as much as possible for herself, even if it takes longer and doesn't get done exactly right.

Toilet Training

This is the age for toilet training. It's true that a few children can be successfully toilet trained in their toddler year. It is more commonly not mastered until the child is nearly three.

You can tell the child is ready to begin toilet training when:

1. The child is dry for long periods of time. The child may show facial expressions indicating she is ready to urinate or have a BM.

2. The child has the language abilities to follow simple instructions: "Point to your hair," "Sit on the chair," etc. and can talk enough to indicate when she needs to be brought to the bathroom or needs help.

Vicki Lansky put together a very good book: *Toilet Training*, that offers many practical tips, and discusses the topic thoroughly. It can be ordered from Practical Parenting, 18326B Minnetonka Blvd., Wayzata, MN 55391.

Needless to say, parents and teachers must work together on the process of toilet training. Procedures and expectations should be consistent at home and at the center. Parents will need to provide training pants and several extra changes of clothes.

Toilet training should be low-key and non-punitive. Expect many accidents at first, and from time to time in the next year. Do not try to toilet train a child who is still adjusting to your program or undergoing some stress like illness or a new baby at home.

Language

What fun! The child begins the year with about 200 words, and by the time she's three generally has command of about 1000 words! She will put together two, three and four word sentences and questions. She will enjoy "chanting," repeating syllables over and over in a sing-song way, and generally playing with sounds.

Most of a two year old's language is either talking to herself, or directed to an adult. What interchanges there are with other children usually involve the territorial imperative: MINE! Get out!

Building vocabulary and language skills should be an important subconscious focus of your teaching. Twos are acquiring skill at a dizzying speed. Do not correct mispronunciations, just model the correct way to say it in a later sentence yourself.

Remember, that children vary widely when they first start

talking, and this is not necessarily a reflection on the child's intelligence.

Shorthand Language

The first short sentences children come out with leave out all the little words. Sometimes this is called "telegraphic speech" because it sounds like the word-efficient telegraphs of the old days. "Daddy fix!" "Me go wif."

Pivot Words

This is when a child takes one key word and attaches many other words to it to make different sentences. "Milk all gone." "Daddy all gone." "Kids all gone." You can expand on this idea with many of his words. When a child comes up with a new word, help him combine it with other words.

Some Tips for Stimulating Language Development

1. Make your language very clear.

    – Be very specific: "Put these red blocks with the other red blocks."

    – Look directly at the child when you are talking to him; watch his eyes and you will know if he is following you or is confused.

    – Be aware of the noise level in the room. A high level of noise is detrimental to language development.

    – Articulate words clearly. *"Let's read that book." "Thank you." "Does the dolly's hat go on her head or on her hand?"*

2. Meet the Match Developmentally

    With the children who have the least productive speech use simple words and phrases for things and actions and increase complexity as the child's language grows. Know where the child is and move forward as he does. Stretch and expand language but don't overwhelm.

3. Teach time and space words.

    Use objects found in the center (blocks, dolls, etc.) to talk about space relationships—in front of, behind, over, under, front, back, etc. Use objects to talk about comparison—which is bigger, fattest, tallest, etc. Which comes first, second, last. Stimulate comparison, judgements, evaluations.

4. Keep talk and attitudes toward language positive. Use praise —but keep it specific. Keep verbal promises. This helps children learn that adult language can be depended upon.

5. Help children learn positive social skills. Teach the magic words of "please" and "thank you" by using these words yourself. Help children to articulate the feelings that they have when someone is rude or kind to them. Model courteous ways of talking with children.

6. Use incongruity — make obvious mistakes. As the children develop language skills, make "silly" mistakes that are obvious. Ask, "Is this my (point to your knee) nose?" Kids love silly things.

7. Read to children in groups and individually. Read something every day. Make up stories to pictures. Create a comfortable book corner.

Poems and Fingerplays

Two year olds enjoy simple fingerplays (poems with simple hand movements). They will often not say all the words with you or do all of the motions, but they seem to like being part of the process and will join you on the emphasis words.

Books

As their language skills increase, simple story books with repeated phrases are fun for two year olds. They also enjoy picture books where they can point to objects and name them.
Some Favorite Books with Repeated Phrases:
Ask Mr. Bear, by Marjorie Flack
Just Me, by Marie Hall Ets
Good Morning Chick, by Mirra Ginsburg
Goodnight Moon, by Margaret Wise Brown
Jump Frog Jump, by Robert Kalan

Conversations

It will be possible to carry on a simple conversation with a two year old. Try to develop the art. Be careful to not only talk "at" children, but to talk "with" them. Listen to what they tell you, and expand upon it. "New shoes." "You got some new pink sneakers! Did your mommy take you to the shoe store last night?"

One way to have good conversations with two year olds is to bring in interesting objects for them to examine and talk about. The food you are having for lunch is always an interesting topic.

A Surprise Bag

Find a special bag that will attract children's attention. A gaudy plastic shopping bag would be good, or a cloth bag sewn from bright material with a drawstring. Let children know this is your "Surprise Bag." Every day, bring in some special object in the bag. It could be an exotic item such as a huge conch shell, or an everyday item like an egg beater. Don't show it to children right away. Put the surprise bag on the shelf and give them time to build suspense and interest. When you take the bag off the shelf children will automatically gather to see what is in it. Then take it out of the bag with a bit of drama, and talk about the object with the children. "What is this? Have you ever seen one? Where do you think I got it? What do you think it is used for?" This is an ideal way to bring in concepts of color, texture, size, weight, etc. By all means, let children handle the object. Concepts become meaningful when children can see, touch, smell and sometimes taste.

Other toys and activities will give you many opportunities to talk to children about what they are doing at the moment and increase their vocabulary and understandings.

Who's In There?

Glue a large picture of a familiar character inside a file folder. On the cover, cut little doors in strategic places. Let the child open the doors one at a time to reveal parts of the picture underneath, and guess who it is. You can

*help provide some language. "Who could this be? Let's
see . . . yellow feathers! Who has yellow feathers? What is
behind this door? Orange feet!"*

*In this fun game the child is also getting some prac-
tice in deductive reasoning, and "part-whole" relationships.*

Time

The child of two has only a vague understanding of time.
"Calendar activities" are not appropriate for this age. They do
not know what a week is or what a month represents. They are
still struggling with yesterday, today, and tomorrow. The names
of the days of the week will have very little meaning to them.
Although they may memorize them by rote, they will not use
them in a meaningful way. Just use the names of the days of the
week in your normal conversation. When children are four they
will be better able to make sense of them. They do know the
difference between night and day.

Number concepts teachers think they are teaching in calendar activities are really beyond most two year olds. Although
some can count by rote, numbers do not yet represent quantities
or sequences for children.

Some things you can do to increase a child's understanding
of time are:

*1. Talk about what goes on during the day. Talk about
what you will do next. When you are sitting at the snack
table, say, for instance, "Soon, when we are through eating we will put our napkins in the wastebasket and wash
our hands. Then we will sit in our circle area and hear a
story about a baby bear." At lunch talk about what happened that morning. Review. Through these discussions
connected to easily recognizable activities, children are
learning the meanings of words such as "soon," "next,"
"first," "before," etc.*

*2. Talk about what you did yesterday, and what will
happen tomorrow. Ask children about what they did last
night.*

*3. Talk about the weather, especially in connection with
words like "today," "yesterday," "last week." You are con-*

necting the passage of time to something more concrete and observable for children.

Music

Singing

Simple nursery rhyme melodies are great for two year olds, as well as other very simple songs such as "If You're Happy and You Know It . . . " and "Row, Row, Row Your Boat." They will now be able to follow along with simple melodies, or at least refrains. Repeat the same simple songs over and over. They enjoy the familiar.

Ring Around the Rosie

This familiar game is a traditional favorite of two year olds. They enjoy being the "rosie" in the middle. Holding hands and walking around in a circle is also fun, and so is falling down together. Not only are they getting experience with music, they are also gaining pleasure at doing things with someone else, being part of the group.

Jenny's Here Today

This little song is sung to the tune of "Farmer in the Dell." Children sit in a circle and one child at a time jumps up and down in the middle of the circle as the others sing, substituting the name of the child in the middle.

"Jenny's *here today,*
Jenny's *here today,*
We all clap together,
'Cause Jenny's *here today."*

Rhythm Instruments

Making an orderly noise with rhythm instruments again gives them pleasurable experiences in being part of a group while being conscious of music.

Clapping Variations

With two year olds, it's best to start out using the body as the first rhythm instrument. Start with clapping. Have children clap softly, loudly, so you can hardly hear it, etc. Then have them try to clap just the way you do. Vary the speed and loudness of your clapping. This exercise will make children focus on you, and gain control of their actions.

Then try the same things, patting other parts of the body. "How does it sound when everyone pats their cheeks?" "Let's all pat the top of our heads at the same time." "Now let's rub our hands together. Now stomp our feet." When everybody does the same action at once, it sounds different from when you do it by yourself.

Now try all these things to music on the record player. With you leading, they may get close to the rhythm of the music. Don't make your expectations too high though.

Instruments

It is good if you can start out with children all using the same instrument at one time. Often a center will not have enough of each type of instrument for everyone to have the same thing. Simple homemade rhythm instruments are fine. One easy favorite is to give each child two empty paper towel tubes to hit together. They make a nice, hollow sound. Let them use the instruments in the ways outlined above before adding music.

It's best to keep rhythm activities like these confined to when children are sitting down in a circle . . . at least at first. Most two year olds are not too successful at walking or "marching" to music while playing an instrument. Too many things to do at once.

Art

Art projects for two year olds are largely exercises in learning to use their hands in purposeful ways. Children enjoy the "cause and effect" of art projects . . . "I move my hand this way, and there is an interesting mark on the paper."

Do not expect two year olds to draw pictures that look like something or put together any recognizable project. If a two year old comes home with a "bunny" or some such thing, pasted together from various pieces of paper, you can be pretty sure that the teacher did most of the process. Very few parents are interested in the level of artistic skill of the teacher!

Scribbling

There is great value in scribbles! First of all, the child is learning to use her two hands for different things simultaneously. She has to hold the paper still with one hand to keep it from sliding around, while making marks with the other hand. Holding onto the crayon and exerting enough pressure to make a mark is another not so easy skill. Eventually the child notices that the mark changes when she changes the pressure of her hand on the paper. Then the child starts to notice the shape of the marks.

A toddler or two year old will start out with mostly horizontal zig-zag marks. Then some vertical marks might intersect. Then the child will start making "round and round" continuous circles. Finally comes the closed circle. When the child makes a closed circle, you know it was a concious, planned thing. Quite an accomplishment, really. But, we are already ahead of ourselves! Circular scribbles don't usually happen before a child is three.

Other Art Activities

Two year olds also enjoy art activities for their sensory pleasures. Colors are pretty to look at. When a child paints with blue paint, she is more likely to remember what "blue" is. Paste feels good when you spread it around, and smells good too. Fingerpaint is wonderful and slippery and beautiful designs appear when you move your hands around. Teachers must accept that children will probably taste all of their art materials. That is why most art supplies made for young children are non-toxic. Make sure that is true for the materials you use!

Concentrate on offering children many different materials to work with. Find different colors, textures, and processes. Don't worry about producing something recognizable. Keep it simple. Some art processes enjoyed by two year olds: fingerpainting; scribbling with crayons, marking pens, chalk; painting at easels with short-handled, wide tipped brushes; tearing paper and pasting pieces; vegetable printing.

Don't try to sit a large group of two year olds down at a table and have them all do an art process at once. You'll be asking for disaster . . . or at least an unsatisfying experience. Instead, present projects to two or three children at a time, while other children are occupied in other activities. With a small group you and the children can relax and talk about what they are doing.

Although children often forget about their art project as soon as they have finished it, parents and grandparents will cherish the masterpieces. Try to save a few before they disintegrate and frame them to send them home to decorate the refrigerator.

What Is Pre-Reading For Two Year Olds?

Similar to toddlers, your main emphasis is on language development and developing a familiarity and love of books as a source of enjoyment.

Although some two year olds, because of parental interest, alphabet books, and educational television are beginning to recognize letters, it does not have a whole lot to do with reading.

When two year olds do such things as play with playdough, make lines and patterns with crayons and paint brushes, and sort shells they are beginning to notice differences in lines and shapes. This is necessary to later noticing the differences in letter shapes.

Location words, "before," "over," etc. are important understandings before children can later make sense of the order of letters and words on a page.

Two year olds should not be "sat down" for specific lessons and drills on letters and the sounds they represent. They have three or four years before kindergarten. There's lots of time for that. If you *really* want to grow "eager readers" just read many fine stories and poems to them, and work on making them skillful at expressing themselves.

Focus

1. Language development is the exciting development this year. An appropriate focus for your planning is providing them varied

experiences to talk about, and giving them the opportunity to talk.

2. Give children many opportunities for parallel play, where they can enjoy doing the same thing as other children, near other children. As they play more and more near or with other children, work on building the word skills to express frustration rather than taking it out physically in aggressive acts.

3. Moving in different ways and trying out all the different things their bodies can do is an interest that can be accommodated indoors and outdoors in games, music and equipment as children develop skill. Also plan many activities that will allow them to practice their developing fine motor skills.

CHAPTER 6

The Three Year Old

Three years old was the age at which traditional nursery schools used to begin to accept children. And with good reason! First of all, most three year olds are toilet trained. The child has survived the turbulence of the toddler and twos years and has turned into a cooperative little person with a sunny disposition who really enjoys being around other children. Three year olds are eager to please and want to do things "right."

People who work with three year olds should enjoy setting up all the traditional nursery school activities, be prepared with a repertoire of fingerplays and children's songs, know how to read children's books to a group, and be ready to listen to children and hear all their excitement. Furthermore, the teacher of threes should enjoy really playing with the children, not just managing them.

Social-Emotional

This is the really exciting development of the year! Three year olds not only enjoy being near other children in parallel play situations, they begin to *interact* with other children in "cooperative play." This is partly because they now have enough language skill to talk and ask questions. It is also because they are gaining an awareness that other people are "real" and have feelings and rights.

It is endearing to see how three year olds can master some of the social graces. "Please," and "thank you," and "let's" are commonly heard, especially if they have good adult models. They are very susceptible to praise. They are friendly and giving.

Taking turns is a new, beginning skill of three year olds. They are beginning to be able to wait a short time for what they want.

Friendships blossom with three year olds. Many children develop a "special friend" whom they seek out in play situations. You will often see three year olds holding hands, or sitting with their arms around each other.

Even though three year olds enjoy the company of other children, they are totally delighted when an adult really plays with them. They are also good at using adults as a resource. Threes will usually not hesitate to approach an adult to ask for help or to show off something new.

Dramatic Play

The housekeeping corner will be a very popular area of your room. In fact, it would be good to make this the *focus* of your room. Give it some extra space and "jazz it up" with interesting materials. It is in this area particularly that children enjoy social contact with each other and can practice the "give and take" of natural social situations.

The "house" is still a good focus for three year olds. They are very familiar with what goes on in houses, and can easily assign roles to themselves. Can you figure out a way to make several "rooms," rather than just having a kitchen? It would be fun to have a bedroom and a living room. Bring in all kinds of "props" to add interest and variety to the play. Such things as placemats, throw rugs, magazines and newspapers, bedding for the doll bed, lunch boxes, and of course dress up clothes and a mirror will add depth and variety to their play. Make sure you allow plenty of free play time when children can develop their own friendships and play partners.

Blocks

The block corner is another place where there is much social interaction and give and take. In fact, it's not a bad idea to have the block corner close to the housekeeping area, because the materials can combine in a natural way.

Wooden unit blocks are fun and exciting for three year olds. When children are first exposed to blocks they may spend much time just lining them up to make "highways" or placing them side by side. Allow this free exploration for quite awhile. Later, the teacher or possibly an older child, can sit down and play with the children, modeling some of the other possibilities of stacking and balancing. Add cars, trucks and small animals and people, and the full range of imaginative play will open up. Is it any wonder blocks are so popular with three and four year olds?

Make sure that you have enough "free play time" in your daily schedule to allow children to practice natural social interactions. "Free play time," called different things in various programs is the block of time in the morning and afternoon when children can choose for themselves where in the room, and with whom they would like to play.

Developing Friendships

Three year olds love having friends. But understand that a "friend" to a three year old is someone who is playing with you right now. Someone with interesting toys or good ideas. That's why when conflict occurs, one so often hears, "You're not my friend anymore!"

Sometimes children need help in learning how to play with

others. Although all three year olds are interested in playing with others and being "friends," some are more skillful than others. You can coach them in these skills, giving them words to enter a play situation, and modelling good play behaviors as you play with them yourself.

Simple circle games, stories, art projects done at a table near other friends, water play around a water table, are all activities enjoyed in the company of others.

Whenever you can free yourself from the "management" responsibilities of the classroom and things are going smoothly, sit down and simply play with children. The presence of an adult will greatly enrich the value of the play as you add language and ideas. Even though threes have a new interest in peers, an adult as playmate is irresistible.

Three year olds, with their new focus on friendships, can sometimes be seen excluding other children from a play situation. "You can't play here. Just Joe and me can play here, right Joe?" This, of course, is painful for the excluded child, as well as for adults watching. Sometimes you can ease the situation by suggesting an interesting role for the excluded child. "It looks like this family needs a big brother . . . ."

Taking Turns

Saying that taking turns is a new skill with three year olds, doesn't mean that they have it mastered. This is a skill that is developed through experience—positive, successful experiences. Teachers will have to guide children in the process. Help children in the dialogue and follow through:

"Jennifer, say, can I have a turn riding the trike?"

"Donna, let Jennifer know when you are through riding in a few minutes."

Giving the child with the wanted toy some control in when to turn it over is usually a good idea. Often, they will do it quite reasonably if they feel they can decide when. Sometimes they will need some gentle pushing. When you suggest it may be time to turn the desired item over to someone new, it may help to have an interesting alternative activity ready for the child who is relinquishing a turn.

"Donna, if you are ready to let Jennifer have the trike, you can come over here and play with Joshua and me. We're painting the building with water."

Sense of Humor

"Slap stick humor" is popular. Three year olds like to laugh at the ridiculous. Accidents will seem funny. They know enough about the world to know how things are supposed to be and look. Variations will interest them. At this point they will laugh both at others and themselves. This can be useful in diffusing situations that could otherwise lead to tears.

Three year olds may start to experiment with silly language, ex.: "Mr. Boo-boo Face." Calling other children names can create problems and hurt feelings. To turn things around, use this characteristic by creating word games. "Boo-boo Face! I thought his nickname was Mr. Lucky Nose! Now, Jenny here is Miss Jump Jump Socks. What is your nickname?"

They also enjoy pronouncing words in silly ways. Nonsense rhymes and other word games will have appeal.

Children enjoy being clowns. Wild, silly gross motor activities have great appeal. Movement and music activities can feed this interest.

Disposition

Three year old children are generally very sunny and agreeable folk. They like to please, and are usually cooperative and eager to do what you suggest.

This is the year when "imaginary companions" appear in the lives of some (not all) children. The child will talk to this companion with great seriousness, and often demand that others acknowledge its presence. Perhaps what we see is the flourishing of imagination, and learning to deal with stress in an abstract way.

This is a common age for fears, especially around 3½. Loud noises, the dark, animals, people or costumed characters may arouse anxiety in children. Children's fears should be taken seriously, not laughed at or brushed aside. Even if we, the adult, know the clown is harmless, the fear is real for the child. When the child senses you are "there" for him, he will be more able to come to terms with what he is afraid of.

You should be aware that sometimes the otherwise sunny three year old goes through a difficult stage at about three and a half. It can be a time of testing, and rebelling. With patience and gentle firmness on your part, the child usually returns to his pleasant self by the time he's four.

Discipline Situations

Three year olds are less likely than two year olds to have a kicking, screaming all-out tantrum.

They are beginning to be able to come up with solutions to problems with other children. Encourage the child to use words instead of physical aggression. At first you may have to model words for them to parrot. "Janie, instead of screaming and hitting, say, "No! I have that now. You can have it in a few minutes." "Marcia, do you hear Janie? She said you can have it in a few minutes. She doesn't like it when you grab."

Three year olds can be obstinate, and may stand like a rock and simply refuse to do something. Try some gentle, positive suggestion techniques and try to avoid confrontations. "Let's do this . . . ," or "How about . . . ."

Knowing their eagerness to please adults and their susceptibility to praise, using "positive reinforcement" can have good effects. Catch a child "doing something right" and notice it out loud. "Laura, you did a good job using words to tell Sean you were mad."

Helping Children Adjust

As with younger children, leaving mother can be hard. Often it helps to try to develop a "secondary bond" with one adult in the classroom first, and then slowly expand the circle to other children. If the same adult greets the child every morning and helps settle him in and is generally "there" for the child, the child can relax and build trust in the new situation and people.

Transitional Objects

   "Transitional objects" such as a blanket or a special stuffed animal a child is strongly attached to can be very helpful, making a child feel more secure in a new environment. By all means, allow children to bring these to the center. These objects will be laid aside by the child eventually when she feels more comfortable.

Physical

   Three year olds are capable of a wide variety of movements.
   They have become quite graceful compared to the top heavy two year old, and they no longer lead with their tummies. Instead of holding their arms out to the side for balance, they swing their arms easily at their side and walk with sureness.

Running seems to be a joy. So is galloping, jumping and "dancing" to music. In fact, threes with their new fluency of movement like to try all kinds of actions. Because of their social nature and their "humor of the absurd" they especially enjoy silly or funny movements.

This is an ideal time to introduce some "creative movement" activities. Since three year olds are newly social, they will enjoy doing movement activities in small or large groups. Possibilities are endless. It's best not to make the activity overly-structured. Encourage their ideas.

Can You Do What I Do?

One favorite "sitting down" follow the leader circle game is to chant:

"Can you do what I do, I do, I do . . .
Can you do what I do, just like me?"

The teacher leads all types of motions such as tapping the top of your head, patting the floor, bouncing your knees, clapping, blinking eyes. Try making children the leader of a motion. Be aware, though, that if you go around the circle, having each child in turn lead a motion, they all may choose the same motion the first leader chose. You might decide that's okay, as long as they're having fun.

One excellent source for movement activities is *Creative Movement for the Developing Child* by Clare Cherry, Fearon Publishers.

This inexpensive book has many movement games to do to simple and often familiar rhymes and music. Often the child is pretending to be something else. All of these things make it perfect for three year olds. The book also follows the developmental sequence from easy movements like creeping and walking to more challenging things like skipping that threes may not have mastered yet. There are good developmental discussions along the way.

Climbing

Three year olds usually alternate feet when they climb up stairs. They may still walk down stairs one step at a time, not alternating feet.

A sturdy climber inside as well as outside will still be very much enjoyed.

Balance Beam

Since most three year olds no longer have that wide stance and their balance is much refined from a year ago, a low "balance beam" presents a challenge they enjoy.

A simple two by four about 4 feet long placed directly on the floor will do. Or you may find more success at first with a plank that is 6 inches wide.

Do balance beam activities in a small group of 4 or 5 children while other children are doing something else so nobody has to wait too long for their turn. Try some of the following motions. At first they may want to hold your hand for security and a little help with their balance.

1. Walk forward across the board.
2. Walk sideways across the board.
3. Walk backward across the board.
4. Walk across the board, on all fours, touching the board with hands as well.
5. Tip-toe across the board, forward and backward.

When this all becomes too simple, use a couple of wooden blocks on either end to raise the board a few inches off the floor.

Tricycles

This is the "Year of the Tricycle!" Some two year olds can master a tricycle, but often it doesn't come until the child is three. A child will typically first propel the tricycle by pushing along with feet on the ground like she did with the wheeled riding toys popular with toddlers and two year olds. What a proud accomplishment when they figure out how to use the pedals! Do make sure the tricycle is the right size so that the child can reach the pedals.

Since very few programs have one tricycle for each child in the program, the much wanted tricycle will also give children much practice in the fine art of taking turns!

Also, since the tricycle usually becomes a car, a fire engine, a motorcycle in the child's mind, it is a prime tool for dramatic play and the exercise of the imagination. If you doubt that, just listen to the sound effects!

Throwing

Children are gaining some basic skill at rolling and bouncing balls, if they have a chance to practice. Catching a ball is still quite difficult, although the child will have occasional success. It is certainly an activity they enjoy. It is a good circle game to bounce or roll the ball to each other.

Bean bag activities such as passing the bean bag around the circle and balancing it on various parts of the body go along with these skills. Threes also greatly enjoy throwing bean bags at a simple target with holes in it. Bean bags may be a bit easier to catch than balls.

Hand Activities

The muscles of the hand are beginning to do what the mind tells them to . . . but they still have a long way to go. For instance, holding a pencil is still very difficult. Three year olds will often hold a pencil, crayon or paint brush with their whole fist.

The "tactile" activities of playdough, clay, water and sand are very popular with three year olds and allow them to practice using their hands in controlled ways. Squeezing, poking and rolling build hand muscle strength. Pouring requires coordination. All of these activities, while providing hand muscle practice also stretch the imagination as the materials take on different shapes.

Cutting

This is the year children usually learn to cut with scissors. Because it is a new skill, it is often very popular. For children who still find cutting difficult, try letting them cut playdough "snakes" as described in the last chapter. This is easy, satisfying, and gives them practice moving their hand muscles in the right way.

It's a good idea to have a "cutting table" set up and available to children most of the time. They start by successfully cutting "fringes" around the edges of the paper. Later they will be able to cut all the way across a piece of paper. Cutting on a line, moving the paper with the other hand, and cutting out pictures from magazines come next. If you have paste and paper handy the cutting experience will be expanded.

Although a dominant hand is not always evident at this age, if a child shows great difficulty learning to cut, you might try offering "lefty" scissors.

A caution—although paper can be difficult to learn to cut, hair seems amazingly easy, and sometimes impossible to resist. Supervise cutting closely with three year olds.

Eye Dropper Color Transfer

   *This activity uses the same muscles as cutting. Fill
an ice cube tray with water. Put red food coloring in a
compartment at one end, yellow in the middle, and blue
in a compartment at the opposite end. Show the child
how to transfer color from one compartment to another
using an eye dropper. Using the eye dropper gives them
practice using their thumb and forefinger together. This
excellent color recognition activity can produce all the
colors of the rainbow, and it will fascinate your three
year olds.*

Manipulatives

   Stringing beads, inlay puzzles, fit together toys, and all the
traditional "manipulatives" find interest with three year olds.
There are many such toys in toy catalogs.
   Three year olds can typically do a three or four piece inlay
puzzle, where pieces combine to make one large picture. As the
year progresses and they gain experience they will advance much
farther, so it's good to have puzzles of increasing difficulty.

Large wooden or plastic beads about an inch in diameter seem to be the easiest for three year olds to handle. Stiffen the ends of the strings with glue or tape. Thin aquarium tubing is also good for stringing large beads. They will also enjoy stringing O-shaped breakfast cereal into necklaces.

Self-Help Skills

It is especially in the self-help routines that we see that three year olds are no longer babies. As the child gains skill in attending to daily routines his sense of independence and self-esteem also grows.

Bathroom Time

Most three year olds are toilet trained and can ask to go to the bathroom. They can wipe themselves. (You may occasionally need to ask parents tactfully to work on this skill with children at home.) Children are usually able to pull their own pants up and down and manage easy zippers and buttons. Some clothing such as overalls may require help. You may wish to encourage parents to dress children in clothing they can manipulate them-selves . . . not so much to save the teacher time, but to allow the child to grow in independence. Even though children are capable of going to the bathroom independently, this activity still needs adult supervision.

Handwashing

Three year olds are quite capable of washing their own hands. Show them how to work the faucets, and make sure they can reach them, how to use the soap dispenser, get the paper towels and dispose of the towel. Make handwashing an integral, automatic part of the child's daily routine after going to the bathroom, after blowing their noses and before eating.

Eating

Children are very capable of feeding themselves at this age. Do not feed children. Do not be fussy about table manners and neatness, and treat accidents casually. Children can serve themselves most foods if you show them how. Although it may be more efficient to dish out food for children, allowing them to help themselves from small serving dishes and pass dishes around gives them a new social skill. They can also learn to scrape their plates and put their plates on a stack. If the adult sets a good model for children manners will come in time.

Dressing

You can expect children to be able to put on their own jackets or coats to go outside. If they do not yet know how, teach them the following nursery school classic:

The Old Coat Trick

1. Place the child's coat on the floor with the neck at her feet.
2. The child stoops down and puts each hand in one of the sleeves.
3. She then picks up the coat and flips it over her head, slipping her arms into the sleeves.

They may need help buttoning or getting a zipper started, but can unbutton and unzip easily.

Children have been able to take off shoes and socks since toddlerhood! At three they can put their socks back on themselves, and can get their shoes on their feet (not necessarily the right ones) but will need help tying shoes.

Let Them Help

Cooperative little people that they are; most three year olds love to help in daily classroom routines. A "helper chart" that rotates jobs among children is found in most classrooms. Some things three year olds can help with, when shown how:

– *setting the table*
– *passing out snacks*
– *folding sheets*
– *putting away nap mats or cots*
– *straightening books on the book shelf*

> — *feeding the classroom pet*
> — *wiping off the table after meals*
> — *putting away toys when it is time to clean up*

It is true that an adult can probably accomplish all of these things more quickly working alone than with the benefit of three year old "helpers." However, speed is not the objective. Allowing children to help makes them feel needed and important, and builds skill in these routines in the process.

Language

Although some three year olds have trouble pronouncing all the sounds of the language, they can generally say what they want to say and have most grammatical structures mastered. Most children who are "late talkers" are spouting forth by the time they are three and a half.

For the first time, children direct speech as much at other children as at the teacher. Their ability to express themselves adequately in most situations is one reason for the blooming of social relationships with other children.

It is not uncommon for three year olds to stutter a little when going through that difficult time at three and a half. As a rule, the less attention paid to a child's stammering, the sooner it disappears. Try to wait patiently for the child to get the words out rather than interrupting and supplying the words. Some parents are anxious about a child's frequent mispronunciations. Some three year olds articulate very clearly, while others persist in "baby talk" pronunciations, although most are still understandable. Again, it's best to relax and wait. Pronunciation will probably clear up by itself within the next year, especially if the child is surrounded by good language models in adults.

Vocabulary Development

Three year olds love new words and they're coming fast and furious at this age. The average 3½ year old has more than 1200 words in his vocabulary. Some of their favorites are "secret," "surprise," "new," and "different."

It's important to keep in mind that children understand a great many more words than they actually speak.

Children learn new words by hearing them in a meaningful context. The best way to increase their vocabulary is to surround them with rich language experiences. Bring in interesting things for children to look at and talk about. Most of all, talk about things they can see or experience right then and there. Notice the weather, the loud truck on the road, the color of someone's new shoes.

Many teachers like to plan learning activities around "themes" or "units." If you do this, you can identify certain words you would like children to understand as a result of the unit, and fir·l pictures, objects and activities that will illustrate the words.

Three year olds can usually understand the space words such as: *on, under, beside, between, back, corner, over, from, by, up, on top of, downstairs, outside.* To strengthen their understanding, here are two fun activities:

Follow the String

Take a long piece of string or yarn around your room, taping it down every so often to hold it in place. Make it go behind, under, over and through objects. Then have children, one at a time, follow the path of the string around the room. While the child does this, you be the "announcer" and describe where the child is: "Zaleb is crawling under the table. Now he is climbing up the steps. Now, down the steps. Now he is going through the tunnel, and there he goes over the chair. Now he is next to the drinking fountain, and here he comes back to us!" Then have everybody clap. You may have to have another adult or older child do this first to give them the idea while you describe the actions. When children have done this activity many times, see if they can take turns being the "announcer," telling where someone else is.

Puppet Directions

Children love to perform for a puppet. Have a puppet tell children to do various things involving location words. "Put the block in the suitcase." "Put the ball behind the chair." "Hold the doll upside down," etc. What might be boring to do for the teacher will be fun to do for the puppet.

Action words and descriptive words are added to children's speech along with names of things as children hear them used in meaningful ways.

Books and Reading

Reading books out loud to children is one of the most important things you can do with three year olds. You are providing several things:

1. Pleasure. You are presenting books as a means for enjoyment. An addiction to books and reading is one of the most valuable gifts adults can give children.

2. Vocabulary Development. Three year olds enjoy new words. Through stories, they will hear new words in a meaningful context and absorb the meanings.

3. Listening Skills. Starting with simple picture books and getting more complex as the year progresses, children will develop the skill to follow the simple line of a story. Their attention span will increase with experience.

4. Stretching Imagination. Books take children out of their immediate environment and into the realm of their imagination.

5. Talk Written Down. As children see a teacher run her finger over the words as she reads, they slowly get the idea that those little black squiggles represent sounds and words . . . a basic pre-reading awareness that is necessary.

What Type of Books?

Three year olds like simple stories about things that are comfortable and familiar, as opposed to scary and exciting. Stories about everyday life, families, the farm, transportation and word books appeal. Books with animal characters are especially popular. They make a familiar situation enough different to be interesting. *Bedtime for Frances*, by Russell Hoban, *Corduroy*, by Don Freeman, and *The Tale of Peter Rabbit*, by Beatrix Potter are examples. Because they also like new words, word books are also popular. Alphabet books may also start to be of interest.

As well as reading at your story time, make books available for children to look through on their own. It's nice if an adult can make herself available to read to a small group of children during the general play time.

Hints on Reading to a Group

1. Timing. When you decide to read to them will make a difference in their ability to listen and enjoy the story. If a child is tired or anxious his ability to relax and concentrate on a story will be decreased. If children have been sitting quietly in activities for a relatively long time, they may need to do a bit of active moving first. If children have been playing actively outside it may take a few "calming" activities to get them ready to sit quietly. Many teachers find several times in their routines when a story is just the right thing. In the morning group time it pulls children together and starts the day on a pleasant note. The right story can be calming before nap time. Late afternoons when toys have been put away is another time books have been helpful. Children can relax and listen and don't have to interact with others.

2. Distractions. It can be difficult to hold children's attention when they can see other children engaged in exciting activities outside or in other parts of the environment. Arrange yourself so their line of sight does not have other distractions. Parents coming in to get children in the middle of a story can also shatter the concentration of the other children. Perhaps you could request in newsletter or other communication to parents that they wait a few minutes until the end of the story when they arrive at that time.

3. Set the Stage. Sometimes it doesn't work well to simply launch into a story once you have gathered children. Try catching their attention with a related object. For instance, finish sewing on a button to a piece of clothing as children watch. Then tell them you know a story about a bear who lost his button, and then take out the *Corduroy* book.

4. Size of the Group. The fewer children there are in the group, the easier it will be for children to concentrate. That is not to say you should not read to your whole group. But when possible, arrange to read to just a few children at a time. When they can snuggle next to you and see you trace your finger over the words while they look at the picture the enjoyment of a story is greatly increased. If there are too many children in the group it will be too difficult for them to see the pictures and not get distracted by

other children. If reading time becomes a battle of getting children to sit still, stop wiggling and kicking, children may begin to view reading as a negative experience.

5. Voice. Keep your voice in a comfortable middle range and be sure you speak loudly enough so all the children can hear you. Change your voice for the different characters in the book to give them more life.

6. Speed. Most people who read out loud to children make the mistake of reading too fast. When you read quickly your voice cannot be as expressive, and take on different voices for different characters. Learn to pause occasionally to add emphasis.

7. Book Selection. Always preread any book you are going to read to your group. Make sure it is a book *you* like to read. If you are bored by a book, this will be transmitted to the children. Judge the vocabulary. It is okay to read books slightly above the level of children. You may want to change some of the words, or shorten the story.

Flannel Board Stories

Although you want to be sure to expose children to many books "straight," telling the story of a familiar book using a flannel board can be a special treat. You are involving children on a different sensory level. Flannel board figures can be made of felt or flannel. You can also cut out paper pictures and back them with felt to use on the flannel board. You could ask children to hold certain characters until it is their turn in the story.

Acting Out Familiar Stories

Children who are very familiar with favorite stories will have fun acting them out with the "directing" of adults. Such stories as "Caps for Sale" by Esphyr Slobodkina, and "The Three Billy Goats Gruff" work very well for this.

Speaking

Much of what we have been talking about has been "receptive language" — understanding. Speaking, or "productive language" is something else.

Unfortunately, studies have shown that there is very little

conversation between teachers and children in some day care centers. The adults speak "at" the children, giving directions and prohibitions, rather than speaking "with" children. Make it a point to converse with each child individually during the day. See how many "turns" back and forth you can reach. In order to encourage children to converse, avoid using only "yes" and "no" questions like, "Did you eat cereal for breakfast today?" Instead, try to ask a content question like, "What did you eat for breakfast?" Ask questions such as, "What do you think is going on in this picture?" Model good conversation skills when you are eating snack and lunch—natural social situations.

Poetry

Don't forget poetry. With their new facility with language three year olds will enjoy learning simple poems and songs. It makes them feel like they are mastering the words and can play with them.

One collection of children's poems with lovely illustrations is *A Child's First Book of Poems* with pictures by Cyndy Szekeres, published by Golden Press.

Finger plays are simple poems accompanied by hand and body movements. These as well as Mother Goose rhymes are greatly enjoyed by three year olds. They enjoy doing the same action as everyone else, being part of the group. There are many collections of finger plays available. One is *Finger Frolics* edited by John R. Faitel, Partner Press, distributed by Gryphon House.

Music

Three year olds are at the point where they can really enjoy singing and other simple music activities.

Wee Sing and *Wee Sing and Play* by Pamela Conn Beall and Susan Hagan Nipp, Price/Stern/Sloan Publishers, are two small books which are collections of many familiar songs and games you will remember from childhood.

Threes can begin to carry simple tunes. Singing along with a group and remembering words to songs are useful exercises in becoming verbally expressive. Most important, they are learning to enjoy the social aspects of music.

Concepts

Although parents and teachers of younger groups surely have touched on concepts, this is a good year to start focusing on the traditional "academic" concepts of color, shape, and size. Try to do this in a "naturalistic" way, building concepts into art activities or simple games you present and normal conversations, rather than isolated "lessons."

Color

Colors are really quite an abstract concept. That's why they're difficult for children until they suddenly "get it."

Teachers have thought of many fun ways to teach colors. Color lotto games are easy to make, and you can use different colors of milk jug tops. Or, glue circles of different colors of paper in the bottoms of muffin tin cups, and let children put matching pom pom balls in the cups. Magazine pictures of certain colors can be cut out and pasted to make a "color poster." Try having a "color week" in which you concentrate on one color all week. Use that color of paint at the easel, make food of that color, ask parents to dress children in that color, etc.

Size

Words describing size are in normal everyday conversation. Try to include such words as you talk to children.

Big and Little Sorting

Collect an assortment of large and small versions of objects — large and small shells, rocks, pine cones, buttons, cans, etc. Let children sort them by size. This could also be done with pictures.

Shape

Shapes are part of our world. There are many ways to point them out to children. Many preschool toys, of course, focus on shapes that you can talk about with children.

Treasure Hunts

Go on a "triangle hunt" or a "circle hunt" around the building and see how many objects of that shape children can find. You can "plant" certain shapes for them to discover.

Shape Collages

Let children make random designs by pasting or gluing an assortment of precut shapes. Or, cut pictures that illustrate a particular shape from magazines.

Letters and Numbers

Children this age can also learn to recognize letters and numbers, and can recite the alphabet and do some rote counting. Follow their interest, but don't press these things too much . . . they still have plenty of time.

Time Words

Abstract concepts of time are quite difficult for three year olds. One reason is that they cannot see time. They do have many time words in their vocabulary like "yesterday" and "tomorrow," but sometimes they confuse these words. "You missed the field trip tomorrow."

"Calendar activities" that give a more visible meaning to concepts of time may be begun this year, in a modest way. Children know about the days of the week, but usually cannot get them in correct sequence. You might have a large calendar with spaces for the days and have a child add a picture each day in the space for that date. That will help them learn the concept of "today" and "yesterday" and "tomorrow." Talk about what you did yesterday, and what you will do today and tomorrow. Adding a weather symbol to each day to show what it was doing outside can also help children begin to understand the passage of time. Threes do not understand ordinal numbers (sixteenth, third, twenty-seventh). Do not spend a lot of time counting up to the date. They may learn the name of the month, but it doesn't mean a lot to them yet.

Art Activities

Three year olds enjoy the whole range of "traditional" nursery school art activities: fingerpainting, brush painting, coloring and scribbling, pasting, gluing, printing and cutting. There are many good "how to" books on art activities for preschoolers that give you exact recipes and procedures. One strong opinion: you should not tell three year olds what to draw or paint or make. Give them the materials and show them how to use them correctly and then let them enjoy themselves, without having to live up to some product assigned by an adult.

Science

What is "science" for three year olds? Up until now, we have not discussed science in relation to a child's development. That is because science is so closely interwoven with everything else. An infant learns about gravity when she throws toys over the side of the highchair tray. Toddlers explore cause and effect. Two year olds busily put descriptive labels on everything they see. The great curiosity of three year olds gives science its own special place in your curriculum.

When you plan science activities, keep in mind that these children do not deal well with abstract concepts. They can only understand what they can see and touch. A focus on animals, nature, and to a certain degree, weather, is appropriate. Don't try to explain air pressure systems, the tilt of the earth and what makes rain . . . they can't touch any of that. Even evaporation is difficult to explain because although they see that the level of the water in the dish is lower, or feel that the cloth is dry, they can't conceptualize the water changing form and disappearing into the air . . . they can't *see* it.

Sorting things, especially objects from nature, is an excellent science activity for three year olds. They must notice details and how things are alike and different. They form mental categories and may start to notice a small part of the "system" of nature. They may be able to notice what objects are made of and sort them accordingly.

The National Wildlife Federation has put out some excellent "kits" of science activities that are just right for three year olds. They are called the *See and Do Nature Series: Animals Up Close*. The kits contain beautiful photograph cards, stories, and suggestions for teachers for expanded games and activities. The same organization also publishes a monthly magazine aimed right at this age group, *Your Big Backyard*. For $8.50 a year, it's a bargain. These materials can be ordered from: National Wildlife Federation, 1412 16th St. N.W., Washington, D.C. 20036.

What Is Pre-Reading For Three Year Olds?

Three year olds can learn to recognize shapes, sizes and colors. They can usually recognize most upper-case letters, but if they don't, don't worry. It's OK to introduce these concepts if you don't "push" them and drill children. Keep it light.

When children sit in a group and listen to a story, they are developing "listening skills." They are learning to focus their eyes on the book, and listen carefully to follow the story line.

The best thing is simply to read to children often and with obvious enjoyment.

Focus

1. Cooperative Play. Three year olds' new skills at interacting with other children deserve special attention. Your dramatic play area could easily be the focal point of your whole room. Set up many activities that are fun to do in the company of others.

2. Language. Blooming language abilities can be nourished through books, games, songs, science and art activities.

3. Moving. Activities that involve moving their bodies in different ways are fun and yet another way to be expressive while developing coordination.

CHAPTER 7

The Four Year Old

"Exuberance." That's the best single word to describe four year olds. Four year olds are enthusiastic, adventurous, bold, "out of bounds," silly, eager, fun. This is the pre-kindergarten year when there is a growing interest in letters and numbers and things academic. But they are not ready to "sit down and behave" for long periods of time. Life is too exciting.

Their interests center around such things as monsters, dinosaurs, and superheroes. They are very imaginative and there is often violence in their imagination. But they also like making faces, singing silly songs and being funny.

People who work with four year olds need to have high energy, a sense of humor and a sense of playfulness. It is important for teachers to be imaginative and creative, enjoy a sense of adventure, and be tolerant of noise and boisterousness. They must also know when to set limits. A tendency toward the dramatic doesn't hurt!

Social-Emotional

Four year olds are outgoing, boastful, but generally polite. They may be jealous of other children who win favor with friends or admired adults. They may sometimes try to exclude another child from a play situation to preserve their social status with the playmate.

Sharing is becoming a bit easier. They are becoming good at negotiating terms. They have less of a need to protect possessions. Cooperative play is blossoming, with much sharing of ideas. There is relatively little solitary play.

The words "out of bounds" to describe four year olds also apply to their emotions. They are expansive, bossy, boasting, and extreme in their emotions. They love things, and hate things with intensity.

Being exuberant and wild, four year olds need limits. You must state clearly what is and is not acceptable. If these limits are reasonable and remain consistent, children usually accept them well.

Aggression

Although aggressive behavior is not uncommon, most of their rebellion is in words. Name calling is not uncommon.

Many teachers are distressed at children's worship of superheroes, and the aggression that can lead to. It is true that television exposes children to a lot of violence on Saturday mornings as well as during prime time. Parents should be encouraged to limit the amount and type of television their children watch, and whenever possible, to watch the show *with* the children so they can help interpret what is going on.

It is interesting to know that part of the interest in violence seems to be developmental. Even if there were no TV, four year olds would still have violence in their imagination and their stories. It has to do with the issue of power. A child this age still feels quite vulnerable and has some fears. If he can identify with a superhero, it is easier to conquer those fears.

Some teachers deal with the superhero issue by emphasizing the positive side of the heroes . . . how they help people and stand for truth and justice and "the American Way."

When aggression does occur, when one child hits, kicks or otherwise hurts another child, this must not be ignored. The teacher must deal with it quickly and clearly. If an adult ignores aggression, children will think that the adult *approves* of the aggression. Even other children in the room not involved in the incident will come to this conclusion.

The teacher should make a very clear statement to the aggressor, something like, "Hitting hurts! It is not OK to hurt people." Do not give double messages — your face and voice should match the message. Be stern without yelling.

Teach children to use words to express their anger. If you can get a child to say forcefully, "That makes me mad!", or "I'm using this now. You can have it when I'm done," or "Stop! I don't like it when you kick me," instead of hitting back, you are making progress.

Children often respond well to the use of "time out" if it is done correctly. Removing the aggressor from the group and having her sit somewhere else for a few minutes can allow the child to "pull herself together" and rejoin the group with more appropriate behavior. The time out should be kept short, usually not more than five minutes or so. The child should not be humiliated, or placed where she is unsupervised, like in a hall or an empty room. Do not label a "time out chair," like a dunce chair. Tell the child, "I want you to sit here for a few minutes and calm down. If you are ready to play without hurting people when I come and get you, you can get up in a few minutes." If possible, involve the child in something totally different when she rejoins the group and give her a clean slate.

It's best not to force four year olds to apologize. If an apology occurs spontaneously and is sincere, that's great. But usually, because a four year old is still very egocentric, the "I'm sorry," is merely a manipulative device to regain favor. If you force it you may just be teaching children to be hypocritical.

Humor

Silliness is often the best way to relieve anger and tension in four year olds before aggression occurs.

Clare Cherry's book, *THINK OF SOMETHING QUIET*, Pitman Learning, Inc., is right on target for dealing with four year olds. The main focus of that book is helping children deal with stress and tension, and it has many good "calming down" activities. She has a specific section on the relaxation of tension through humor, featuring that old classic song, "The Bear Went Over Banana." Who could resist!

Swear Words

Experimenting with swear words and "bathroom words" is also enormously interesting to four year olds. Some behaviorists will tell you to ignore the behavior and it will go away. This may be the best course of action. However, it will not always work. Other children may still react and reinforce the behavior.

You might try launching into an intellectual discussion. "Isn't it interesting that certain sounds make people so upset?" One way to negate the negative impact of swear words in the classroom is to make up your own silly swear words. Then pretend to be offended and shocked when they say them. "Did you hear that!!! He called me a snickelnose!!!"

Or you may just give the matter of fact statement, "We don't want you to use those words here."

Imagination

At four the imagination of children is flourishing. They love adventure, excitement, excursions, anything new. Children three and under have been pretty busy just figuring out how the world works, and the flexibility in their thinking has been limited. But by now, the child has had enough experiences with the world to sense its infinite possibilities. Their imagination shows up in much of what they do.

Dramatic Play

This vivid imagination feeds dramatic play of all types. You see it everywhere with four year olds, in planned and unplanned situations.

The "house corner" with child sized furniture, dolls and dress-up clothes remains one of the favorite places in the pre-school classroom, as it was when the child was three. But their play has become more elaborate. Where three year olds were fairly rigid in the family roles assigned, four year olds can think of many more roles to play.

Four year olds will also greatly enjoy pretend play in different "settings." Use furniture, boxes and props to create such settings as restaurants, television studios, busses, airplanes, rocket ships, the seashore, the post office, beauty shops, and a campsite. If you plan activities around a theme unit, you can almost always think of dramatic play opportunities to enrich the unit.

It is important to keep in mind that boys enjoy fantasy play just as much as girls. Dress-up clothes and props should accommodate the male roles as well as female roles. There are some boys who never seem to want to play in the house corner. Perhaps some subtle early social conditioning has already taken hold and they don't want to be caught playing with dolls. Where do they choose to play instead? Usually in the block corner where they become construction bosses, highway engineers, and giants . . . still very much in the realm of fantasy play! When play settings are varied as described above, we usually see eager participation from boys as well as girls.

You see dramatic play everywhere the child plays. A tricycle becomes a car, an ambulance, a fire engine. A climber turns into a rocket ship, a burning building, a cage in the zoo. A crayon becomes a race car zooming around the paper track.

What is the Value of Dramatic Play?

Most people are quite accepting of house play with three year olds. In this "push your child" age, however, one hears more and more pressure to get the pre-kindergarten child to abandon fantasies and "get down to the business of learning." What a mistake this would be! Time spent pretending is time well-spent!

The social advantage of pretend play with other children, of course, continues. In the give and take without adult intervention or leadership, children sort out who they are and how to get along with others.

The word, "imagination," shares a root with the word "image." If a child can imagine himself as big and capable and act it out often he is more likely to become big and capable. Through fantasy play, the child rehearses life experiences and roles.

A child with a rich experience in fantasy play develops flexibility in thinking, and is better able to cope with change and stress in later life. The outward dramatic play of the child becomes the daydreaming and private fantasies of adults. One must first imagine oneself in a better situation before being able to take action for change.

Children sometimes play out an unpleasant or frightening experience of real life. In the process they gain control of their fears.

Physical

Four year olds are expansive in their movements. They run fast, climb high, gallop, jump and hop. There seems to be energy and "push" behind everything they do. A very "physical" age!

This is the age when people are most likely to label a child "hyperactive." Often, upon closer examination, it will turn out that the child is simply exhibiting the high energy typical of the age and is not provided with enough outlet for this energy. It's when adults expect four year olds to sit still for too long that trouble brews.

A discussion of the physical characteristics of four year olds must include how to handle this high energy load.

One solution is to provide ample outdoor time, when they can engage their loud voices as well as their muscles for running and climbing. A playground with a good climber and space to run and ride tricycles is invaluable. Circle games, follow the leader games, "chases," monster play, are all fun outside.

The main trick is to determine how much out of bounds behavior you can allow, and when to put the lid on. Don't make everyone's life impossible by expecting four year olds to sit still for long periods of time. Build in plenty of relaxed play time when children can play at their own energy level. It may help to have a very vigorous activity just before you want them to settle down for awhile, to "get the wiggles out." Relax and enjoy it when you can. Take part in the silliness.

Bad Weather Survival

Nobody watches weather forecasts with greater interest than a teacher of four year olds. Bad weather survival is an important skill of people who work with this age group.

The balloon tennis game described in the chapter on two year olds will still be greatly enjoyed by four year olds. (Outside, you can try using badminton birdies rather than balloons.) Dancing while waving around long crepe paper streamers will use up energy inside. Having target practice with the "soft balls" made from nylon stockings and polyester fiberfill stuffing is fun indoors. Here's another favorite energy absorbing game:

Skizamaroo

Children stand in a circle and chant while jumping and clapping their hands:

"Skizamaroo and Timbucktoo,
I can do anything you can do!"

A "leader" then demonstrates any kind of motion, and the others imitate it. It's fun to add a sound with the motion. Then they go back to the jumping chant and go to the next person in the circle to be the leader and demonstrate a different motion to copy. Go all the way around the circle.

Add other things to your "Rainy Day" kit like special board games, dress-up clothes, and art materials that may only be brought out when it rains and you can't go outside. Who knows? You and the children might even look forward to rainy days!

Other Gross Motor Activities

Four year olds enjoy any activity that allows them to use their muscles. Creative movement and dancing are great fun. They enjoy all kinds of circle games, as long as they don't have to wait, doing nothing until it is their turn. Throwing and catching balls, activities with bean bags, parachutes, hoops, and ropes will all attract much interest and eager participation.

Fine Motor Activities

Fours are getting skillful at using their hand muscles. They can button, zip, lace shoes, but usually not tie shoes, string small beads, cut with scissors, pour juice.

Games and toys with many little pieces are popular. Lacing cards provide a challenge. They like to build with cubes, put together puzzles, play with tinker toys, draw, color, and print the letters of their names. Simple jigsaw puzzles will challenge some children more than the typical wooden inlay puzzles. Small plastic pattern blocks, various construction toys and using wooden peg boards and small pegs will attract the interest of four year olds.

Stringing Straws

Cut up plastic drinking straws into small sections of one-half to one inch. Children will enjoy stringing these to make necklaces. Unlike bead necklaces, they can take these home.

Self Help Skills

Like three year olds, but more so, four year olds really love to be very helpful in daily routines, and generally enjoy feeling important and useful.

If you put juice and milk in small pitchers, children have reasonable success pouring their own drinks. (Provide valuable practice in your water play activities.) Have a sponge handy and show children how to clean up their own spills.

They generally do just fine feeding themselves. Model good manners, but do not harp on them. Exuberant and silly four year olds often pick mealtime to imitate each other, make faces and play with their food. Certainly, it is appropriate for the adult to put a limit on this. That is one good reason teachers should sit down at the table and eat with four year olds, more or less guiding the discussion in a different direction when it starts to get out of hand.

Almost all four year olds have mastered the entire routine of going to the bathroom. You will probably have to give frequent reminders about handwashing.

But that is not the major problem. Four year olds need supervision in the bathroom because they are very interested in bathrooms in general, and other children in particular. Silliness and "bathroom talk" is very typical. It is the prime age for "you show me yours, and I'll show you mine." Although this curiosity is natural, the child care center is not the appropriate place for gaining information. If you do happen upon children engaged in exploratory behaviors, put a stop to it in a matter of fact manner.

Most four year olds are quite skillful at dressing themselves. They can button most buttons, zip up and manage a belt buckle. Tying shoes is still beyond most children. Velcro shoe fasteners to the rescue!

A Grooming Center

Set up a mirror in your room and have a comb or brush for each child, with his name on it. These could be stored in shoe bags. Encourage children to wash their faces and then comb their own hair after getting up from nap or coming in from outside.

Need for Rest

It is often at the age of four and a half or slightly later that some children have real trouble settling down and falling asleep at naptime. And yet, if they do not rest well in the middle of the day, the afternoons can be rough. There are some four year olds who simply cannot fall asleep, yet the high energy demands of this age really need to be met by a period of rest. Non-sleepers should not be forced to lie quietly on a cot or mat for the entire nap period while other children are sleeping. This is as close to torture as you can get for a high-energy four year old, and could make him hate coming to the center. A good solution is after a reasonable time of lying quietly and trying to sleep — a half hour or 45 minutes — to allow the child to get up and engage in some quiet activities such as looking at books, listening to story records using head phones or playing with legos . . . in another room, if possible.

It will be to your advantage to calm children down as much as possible before naptime. It can start before lunch. Pull kids together after an active morning with a short group discussion that recaps the morning and looks forward to the afternoon. A good story fits in nicely here. Lunch should be pleasant and unrushed. Start talking in a quieter voice. Anticipate naptime pleasantly. "Ah, soon we'll be able to stretch out on our cots and close our eyes and relax." Yawn a lot. When everyone is lying down is another ideal time for a story, especially if you tell the story rather than read a book. Tell them to see the pictures in their imagination. Take care not to make the story too exciting or you'll have them all revved up again! Deep breathing, soft music, lullabies, back rubs, help too. (Sounds great, doesn't it?)

Language

Four year olds generally have a lot to say. Most of their language is now directed at other children rather than at adults, although they are good at asking adults for help. They can sustain play with other children for as long as 20 or 30 minutes with good reciprocal conversation throughout. They like to give information, and greatly enjoy some one-on-one talking time with favorite adults.

Four is a noisy age . . . they are loud in almost everything they do. Teachers of four year olds are often heard admonishing: "Use your indoor voices."

The silliness and expansiveness of a typical four year old's personality, of course, carry over to language. Most four year olds have become quite facile with language, and now they can afford to fool around with it. They enjoy playing with words and making up new, funny words and sounds. They love exaggerations and words like, "enormous," "gigantic," "colossal." They enjoy extremes in their voices, shouting, whispering, and telling "secrets."

This is also known as the age of "Why?" Sometimes the why's are a genuine quest for information about the infinite mysteries of the universe . . . and sometimes they are simply a ploy to extend the attention of the adult. If you make a thoughtful attempt to answer the incessant questions you are likely to encourage an inquiring mind. Don't hesitate to say, "I don't know." Also ask, "What do you think?" "Let's find out," is another wonderful response.

Books

Whereas three year olds like nice, gentle books about families, animals and familiar things, four year olds like books that are adventurous or silly. Books about giants, monsters, dinosaurs, animals in people roles and machines have great appeal. Maurice Sendak's *Where the Wild Things Are* is a bit too threatening and scary for three year olds. It is, however, the all time favorite for four year olds. Poetry, especially funny poetry, will catch their interest.

Four year olds enjoy complexity in illustrations in their books. They like to search for a small object on a page and gaze at the beautiful colors and patterns of well done art work.

Story Telling

Four year olds now have enough language comprehension that they can enjoy a story that is *told* without a picture book, rather than read to them. To follow the story they have to rely only on the spoken words, without any visual clues.

You might start out with easy stories about the children themselves in familiar surroundings: "Once upon a time there was a class of children, and they had the most wonderful teacher in the world. First thing in the morning two fine boys came in the room. Their names were Caleb and Scott. Scott said . . . let's feed the rabbit . . ." and you go ahead and relate the events of the morning in your own room. They will listen with rapt attention, filling in on some of the details as you go.

Later you can go on to more traditional stories like "Little Red Riding Hood" or your own made-up fairy tales.

Fill-in-the-blank stories

Children are especially good at this if you have read many stories to them. You supply connecting phrases, and they fill in the colorful and exciting details. The point is not for the child to retell a familiar story, but to make up a new story. Any fill-in word that fits the context of the teacher's preceding phrase acceptable. In the process, children not only exercise their imagination but get valuable experience in listening, logical thinking and the context of language. This is great fun to do with a small group.

Teacher: "Once upon a time there was a . . .

Child: Bear!

Teacher: This bear was very, very . . .

Child: Big.

Teacher: In fact, this bear was so big, that he couldn't . . .

Child: fit in his cave.

Teacher: 'Oh dear,' said the bear . . . 'what shall I do?' He sat down and started to . . ."

etc. etc. etc.

These stories can be wonderful fun and allow the expansive imagination of a group of four year olds to really take off. It's fun to tape record these stories and later transcribe them into a book.

Child-dictated stories

Invite a child to tell you a story. A child is often so pleased at the undivided attention of an adult that he will eagerly comply. To extend the child's use of language, you might offer some questions: "Then what happened?" "Was she afraid?" "Did anyone come along?" Tape recording these stories adds importance to them and children will enjoy listening to them again and again.

Art work is often accompanied by spontaneous stories or explanations. Grab a pencil and write the words down as the child dictates . . . but hang onto your hat and don't be surprised at the violence that emerges: ". . . and then the monster came along and bashed his head in . . ." That's typical of four year olds. Write it down without judgmental statements. The child is learning about the power of words.

Here is a story enticed from a group of four year olds sitting around a lunch table one day. It started with Manfred's statement, "I was here last night." The teacher said, "Wait a minute, let me get a pencil . . . this sounds good." Writing the words down gave them added importance and other children joined in to add details.

GIANT IN NIGHT

"Last night when nobody was here, Manfred went to Christopher's, Tommy's, Justin's and Jimmy's house and got them. They came to school and snuck in. Nobody came after them. First they went to Debby and Doris's room, and messed it up. Then they cleaned up the room so nobody would know. Then they came to our room.

Then a man came and captured them and put them in a cage! (He was a giant.) Tommy reached the key in the giant's pocket and gave it to Manfred who unlocked the cage and let everyone out. Then they all kicked the giant and threw coffee in his face and he died.

Then a picture fell off the wall and they cleaned up the glass with a magic broom.

Manfred drove everyone home on his motorcycle except Christopher, who followed very fast on his tricycle (which is faster than any car.)

They climbed back in their windows, changed back into their pajamas and went back to bed.

Their mommies didn't even know they were gone!

THE END

Language Games

I Spy

This familiar guessing game is fun to play with four year olds. "I see something in this room that's made of plastic and it's round, and you blow it up, and it has yellow, blue, red, and white sections and it bounces." Children must not only use their listening and comprehension skills but also their deductive thinking skills in eliminating possible answers one by one.

After children have a lot of experience playing this game with the adult as the leader, let them take on the challenge of being the person to describe the mystery object. That takes real skill in producing the right words, and deciding what to say about an object without naming the object.

Banana Fanna

Here's a word game that allows children to play with sounds. A group of children recites the basic chant together, substituting names of different children in the group.

The skeleton of the chant looks like this:

_____ bo b _____
Banana fanna fo f _____
Me, my, mo m _____
_____

some examples:

Erik, bo berik
Banana fanna fo ferik
Me, my, mo merik
Erik!

Joshua bo boshua
Banana fanna fo foshua
Me, my, mo moshua
Joshua!

Shirley bo birley
Banana fanna fo firley

Me, my, mo mirley
Shirley!

Get it? Four year olds catch on to this amazingly
quickly!

Lotto Games

Lotto games are basic picture matching games with good opportunities for vocabulary development and comprehension. Typically, there will be a large card with several pictures on it, and small cards with individual pictures which match those on the card. It is usually played with several players, but can be done as an individual matching game.

Lotto Game Skill Progression:

1. Simple Matching

You are working on the concept of "same and different" here. You show the child a small card and say, "Is there a picture on your card that is the *same* as this? You can help the child make the judgment by holding the small card next to the pictures on the card and compare details.

2. Show a card to the children and ask, "What's this?" Have the child produce the word. "That's right, this is a wagon. Do you have a wagon on your card?"

3. Describe what is on the small card without showing it to the children. "This is a piece of fruit that grows on a tree. It is red. When you bite it, it crunches. Sometimes we drink juice made from this fruit." Children must understand your words and get a visual image in order to make a match.

Simple Ways to Make Lotto Games:

Although there are many lotto games available to purchase in stores and catalogs, it's fun to make your own. You can then "tailor make" them to match the special interests of your children.

Magazine Lottos

Buy two copies of the same issue of a magazine. Cut the same pictures out of each. Glue one of each onto a large card, and one onto a small card. Large cards can have four to six pictures on them. Cover all the cards with clear contact paper for durability. Four year olds love cars and trucks, so magazines focusing on cars would be great.

Wrapping Paper Lotto

Wrapping paper, because of the many seasonal and child-oriented themes, is often ideally suited to be made into lotto games. Some wrapping papers present a "busy" picture with similar objects on it. Individual items can be cut out to match, the small cards following the contour of the drawings rather than being rectangular. This provides an excellent visual discrimination exercise. Since a lot of wrapping paper features funny characters it will appeal to four year olds.

Stamp or Sticker Lotto

Nature stamps or stickers provide fun and easy ways to make lotto games.

Different Types of Lottos:

Category Matching

Put different categories of pictures on each large card. For example, mammals on one, birds on another, fish on a third, and reptiles on a fourth. Children are therefore forming mental categories as they are matching cards. Other possible categories: tools, toys, cars, trucks, airplanes, boats, food, flowers, trees, etc.

Go Together

The child must match up pictures on the large card and small cards that are not the same, but go together such as a toothbrush and toothpaste, soap and a washcloth, car and car keys, horse and saddle, etc.

Environments

The large card will have a picture of a room or scene

on it. Small cards will be small details cut from those scenes. Children will look at a picture of a toaster, for instance, and decide it is more likely to go in the kitchen card than in the forest card or the bedroom card. Again, magazines are good sources for pictures.

Puppets

Four year olds, with their capable imaginations and growing abilities to produce language, have fun with puppets. They will not put together elaborate plays or even dialogues with other puppets, although there may be some play between puppets.

Puppets allow children to take on silly voices, to roar, to pretend to bite, to sing silly songs. In other words, puppets allow children an outlet for many of the things that are typical of being four year olds . . . which may not always be considered socially acceptable for real people to do.

If a teacher has a "pet puppet" or two with special personalities and voices, children will be even more resourceful in their use of puppets the teacher makes available to them.

Homemade puppets are just as good as (and often better than) purchased puppets. You don't need a puppet stage, although children will enjoy using a large box turned into a theater. The book, *Puppetry in Early Childhood Education* by Tamara Hunt and Nancy Renfro, published by Nancy Renfry Studios, gives you many ideas and techniques for using puppets as well as imaginative ideas for making these valuable classroom friends.

Group Discussions

Four year olds have the attention span for brief group discussions, especially if they are interesting.

"What would you do if . . ." discussions can be successful with four year olds. "What would you do if you got lost in the supermarket?" Use this also for fun with imaginations. "What would you do if you found a talking toad on the playground?" "What would you do if you suddenly discovered you could fly?"

Sometimes the books you read children can be the starting point for discussions. "Have you ever seen a steam shovel like Mike's?" "What was it being used for?" . . .

In your discussions with children, try to keep a good portion of your questions "open-ended." Don't just ask questions that have one right answer, or a "yes" or "no" answer. Example of a closed question: "What was the dog's name?" (The answer will either be the right name or a wrong name, or an "I don't know.") Example of an open question: "What would you do if a dirty dog like Harry ran in the house?" (any answer acceptable).

Show and Tell

Show and tell, the old nursery school classic where one child at a time stands up and shows some object brought from home and talks about it, is designed to give children experiences in speaking in full sentences and sharing ideas in front of a group. Often this activity turns out less than ideal. Many times it seems to be a session of "bring and brag" instead of show and tell as children try to outdo each other with their superhero toys. I have also seen a normally exuberant child stand up in front of friends she plays with every day and stare at her feet, unable to utter a word. It seems too young to suffer the agonies of stage fright! Then there are always the children who want to dominate and go on and on. Other children find it very hard to wait their turn. Perhaps it is too forced.

There are some good variations. If it is more spontaneous it seems to work well. A child comes in with a box of new kittens. Now, *that's* something to talk about! If children are made to feel that they can tell the group about something interesting any time it is more natural. Some teachers limit show and tell to one day a week, and ask parents to help children find something that relates to the "unit" or "theme" they are working on. That makes sense for parent involvement and extending learning. One teacher has a "Nature Show and Tell." Children may bring in objects for the science table and talk about where they found it, what it is, etc.

Calendar Activities

Four year olds understand many space words and comprehend most concepts of time. This is the year when it makes sense to spend time on "calendar" activities to reinforce these concepts.

Blocks

Wooden unit blocks and large hollow blocks are greatly enjoyed by four year olds. Combined with cars and trucks, plastic dinosaurs, plastic zoo or farm animals, and little people, children use blocks to create scenes for their imaginations. If the teacher also plays with blocks from time to time and models interesting ways to build, the imaginative use will be even greater.

A great deal of language skill is developed in the block corner. There's the oral communication as children explain their structures and develop imaginative play around trains, airports, hotels, etc. The following activities are ways in which the teacher can structure block play to develop an understanding of shape, size, number, and similarities and differences.

Use All the Blocks

After your children have had much experience playing with blocks they enjoy this different challenge. Tell

*them to see if they can use all the blocks on the shelf in a
given period of time. Set the timer.*

Same Blocks, Different People

*Give two children exactly the same number and
shape of blocks. Tell them to make something with the
blocks, but don't let them see each other as they build.
When they are both finished have children see how similar or different their constructions are.*

Exact Copies

*Give two children exactly the same number and
shape of blocks and tell them to make buildings that are
exactly the same. They will really have to work together
closely and notice shapes and sizes!*

The large hollow blocks can be made into something "huge"
(a favorite word). Usually building something with large blocks
is a cooperative effort with other children. They are great for
stretching the imagination.

Music

Four year olds like to sing and they especially enjoy silly
songs. *Wee Sing Silly Songs* by Pamela Conn Beall and Susan
Hagen Nipp, Price/Sloan Publishing, is a collection of many of
the funny songs you remember from childhood.

The loud noises of rhythm instruments are also very appealing to fours. How about a rhythm band parade around the playground, flag and all? Dancing and moving to some of the excellent early childhood music records on the market is also a popular activity with four year olds.

Science

This is the "Why?" age, remember? What could be more perfect than science activities as a strong focus for your planning?

Like three year olds, fours still have a hard time dealing with abstract concepts or things that they cannot see, so stay away from explanations that go beyond what children can see and touch. But, do help them to see *more*. They are interested in what is real and what is not real. They want to know what's inside of things . . . like rocks. They want to see the back side of everything. They may get interested in what "dead" is when they see a dead animal on the road. Keep a piece of fruit or your Halloween pumpkin around (in a covered container) and let mold grow.

Studying about dinosaurs is the all time favorite science unit for four year olds . . . of course! They love pronouncing the long names, and discussing how huge and dangerous they were. There are quite a few good dinosaur books for preschoolers on the market.

Be spontaneous in your science investigations. Follow the questions of four year olds.

Art

It is in this year that children usually begin drawing things to look like something. Three year olds mainly scribbled, or at most, made circles with faces in them. Four year olds will typically start "doodling," making random lines on the paper, and then suddenly notice that the lines resemble something. Then they will add details and tell you a wild story about it! Still refrain from telling children what to draw. Let the ideas come from them.

They will greatly enjoy the whole range of art projects. Focus on giving them many different materials to work with and let them explore their possibilities.

What Is Pre-Reading For Four Year Olds?

This pre-kindergarten child is becoming interested in naming letters and sometimes picking out words she knows. Don't force this on children in large doses, but if the interest is spontaneous, encourage it. Many four year olds will pretend to write letters and read books. Activities focusing on color, shape, location and numbers are also appropriate for this age.

Listening skills gained in group activities and enjoying books are a major part of being ready to learn to read.

The main "danger" with four year olds is that the teacher, sensing their abilities, will "over-do" it, and put too much focus on trying to teach children to read. It is very hard for energetic four year olds to sit quietly doing "seat work" for very long. Use active games and activities to teach concepts and stay tuned-in to their energy level and interest. Be careful not to turn learning to read into a negative thing.

Focus

IMAGINATION. This word says it all. In all of your activities, be they art, science, children's literature, movement, dramatic play or blocks, the imagination should be dominant. If you can encourage and stretch the natural imagination and curiosity of four year olds and not squelch them, you are giving the child a valuable gift and tool for later life. You will have created "eager learners," children who want to know more.

Learning to recognize letters and numbers, shapes, sizes and colors can be a secondary focus, preparing children for the kindergarten year ahead.

CHAPTER 8

The Five Year Old

Whereas the four year old was wild and out of bounds, the five year old is composed and "together." The typical five year old is calm, serene, wants to be good, and generally looks on the sunny side. The five year old loves to be read to and talked to and likes to learn new facts . . . ideal for kindergarten!

A teacher of five year olds should be able to blend "academic" learning of math and reading skills with a sense of order in the room, still allowing for spontaneity, creativity and fun.

Social-Emotional

The five year old is generally a very pleasant person to be around. He likes to help, and loves praise. He has ideas and loves to talk about them. He can judge pretty well what he can and cannot do, and is fairly self-limiting.

Some children go through a difficult period at around five and a half when they may become brash, disobedient, over-demanding and explosive. These children may also tend to dawdle, and be less coordinated than they were before. It usually doesn't last long if treated with patience and understanding.

They usually respond well to praise and empathetic listening. A short time apart from other children to pull themselves together again often helps when a child is having trouble controlling himself.

Taking things that belong to others and then lying about it is one of the more common behavior problems among five year olds. Because they want so much to be good, it is hard for them to admit when they have slipped up.

Five year olds are often extremely fond of their teachers.

Cooperative Play

"Cooperative Play" is the norm for five year olds. They usually prefer playing with one or more other children to playing by themselves. They assign roles, "set the scene," get ideas from each other and can get quite involved in their play scenario. This is most obvious when they are involved in dramatic play in the dress-up corner. But it happens outside on the climber and on wheeled toys, while playing with blocks, and while building with construction toys as well.

Children doing art projects will engage in pleasant social conversations while sitting at the same table with others.

It is distressing to see kindergarten programs which are so "business like" or limited for time that they think blocks, dress-up play and outside play are a waste of time. It is in these activities that children's imaginations flourish, providing them ultimately with a greater flexibility in thinking and coping skills.

Physical

In contrast to the expansive four year old, the five year old is poised and controlled. Arms are generally held close to the body.

All kinds of movement activities and dance usually appeal to this age group. Skipping is a new skill for five year olds. They may even enjoy learning some simple dance "routines." Encourage them to make up their own routines and teach them to their friends.

In playing with a ball, boys and girls have developed their characteristically different style of throwing. Boys will throw a ball with a sideward stroke of the arm, and girls throw overhand. Depending on the amount of experience they have had, both boys and girls can be fairly successful at catching a medium sized ball.

Tricycles and other wheeled riding toys are still fun. There are some fine riding toys designed for cooperative play that have great appeal for five year olds.

Hand Coordination

By five, it is usually evident whether the child is right-handed or left-handed. Do not try to force a left-handed child to use his right hand for writing and drawing. Have left-handed scissors available to avoid frustration for the left-handed child.

Writing

Children this age are ready to begin printing letters on lined paper, although for some it is still very difficult.

A five year old can hold a pencil correctly when shown how and likes to make lines, letters, and drawings. Provide a variety of writing and drawing implements such as colored pencils, ball point pens, fine line felt tipped markers and crayons to encourage children to practice this skill.

Coloring

Five year olds are gaining skills at coloring within outlines.

Rather than using coloring books, which may inhibit creativity, give the child cookie cutters, stencils or templates to trace around and then color within the lines. He will enjoy making various patterns and designs, and his creativity will be encouraged rather than stifled.

Manipulatives

Lacing cards, puzzles with many pieces, sewing with large yarn needles and burlap in hoops, making patterns with small colored pegs and peg boards, and fit-together bricks are all popular with five year olds, and let them practice their eye-hand coordination, and making patterns.

Self Help Skills

Some, but not all five year olds can tie their shoes. Most can button, and zip jackets with bottom opening zippers.

Language

Books

All kinds of books are interesting, especially humorous story books, books where animals take on the roles of people, and factual books that tell them about their world.

Some Favorite Books

Alexander and the No Good, Very Bad Day, by Judith Viorst.

Be Nice to Spiders, by Margaret Graham Bloy

Whistle for Willie, by Ezra Jack Keats
The Dead Bird, by Margaret Wise Brown

All Kinds of Families, by Norma Simon
Bodies, by Barbara Brenner
Madeline, by Ludwig Bemelmans

Discussions

The language skills of five year olds are well developed and they enjoy talking about a wide range of subjects.

News Board

Often children will come in in the morning bursting to tell you something. "My grandfather came to our house for a visit! He came on a train!" Establish a "news" bulletin board for such items. Then you can say, "That sound's like something for our news board. Let's write it down." Let the child dictate the words to you. You might invite him to draw a picture to go with it. Then post it on the board. During your group time, have any children who have posted news items read them, or tell about them, to the rest of the class. This process has allowed the child to "rehearse" his words, and it is a pre-reading exercise.

Poetry

It's a lucky child who has a teacher or parent who can share with the child the love of poetry. The surest way to kill an interest in poetry is to force children to memorize and recite it. On the other hand, if a teacher shows obvious enjoyment of the poem herself, it will be contagious. "I came across this poem that I like a lot, and I wanted to share it with you."

One favorite collection of poems and activities is *Imagine That,* by Joyce King and Carol Katzman, published by Goodyear Publishing Co., 1976. This is actually a "curriculum book" that builds creative activities around poems. It would be very good for pre-kindergarten classes as well as kindergarten classes.

Five year olds are beginning to have the sophistication, the vocabulary and the ability to play with words that will allow them to enjoy the wonderfully funny poetry of Shel Silverstein in his collections, *A Light in the Attic* and *Where the Sidewalk Ends,* published by Harper and Row. Although there are a few poems in this collection that will appeal to four year olds, generally there is a level of sophistication and subtlety that will escape four year olds. Not all of the poems will be right for five year olds, for that matter. Pre-read them and judge.

Drama

Like four year olds, fives will enjoy a wide range of dramatic play opportunities. Develop "props" to represent many different roles for children to act out in spontaneous dramatic play.

They will also enjoy acting out familiar stories and putting on simple plays. You could make stick puppets to represent the characters of a familiar story. Children could hold them up as you read, when that character talks in the story. Then let children act out the same story using their own bodies rather than puppets.

Learning to Read

Many five year olds have the aptitude to start to learn to read. Most kindergarten programs use a structured reading program. Pre-kindergarten programs, on the other hand, usually teach concepts through more active games and activities. Don't push, though. It won't hurt to wait awhile, and it's best not to frustrate a child. (Children who learn to read later usually catch up with other children by second or third grade.)

Worksheets

Dittos — worksheets — workbooks — coloring books — reproducible patterns—are all inappropriate for preschool classrooms. (Preschool is defined as anything under kindergarten level.) For that matter, they're not great for kindergarten either and should be used only in a limited way to provide "drill" for concepts already learned. There are much more effective alternative ways of teaching young children.

Objections to Worksheets

Here are the main objections to using worksheets with children under kindergarten level:

1. Children this age do not understand abstract concepts well. Letters, numbers and shapes on a piece of paper are abstract symbols representing something else that is real.

2. Children learn basic concepts by using all their senses, by manipulating objects. They will not learn anything *new* with worksheets. At most, worksheets will provide "drill" for concepts already learned.

3. Children under kindergarten age don't have the fine-motor control to color within the lines, or do many of the other tasks often asked on typical worksheets.

4. "Seat work" — sitting at a table doing worksheets is hard enough for kindergarten and first grade students. Younger children have a shorter attention span and find it difficult to sit still for more than a few minutes at a time.

5. Worksheets are not fun . . . not for long anyway. As soon as the fascination of "playing school" wears off they become drudgery. (Think back to your own days in elementary school. Very few adults remember loving to do workbook pages.) We want to make children eager, enthusiastic learners, not people who avoid learning situations.

6. Worksheets do not develop creativity. In some cases they may actively inhibit the creative process in children. When children are given patterns to copy or color in they become less likely to come up with their own ways of drawing things.

7. Teachers sometimes use worksheets merely to "occupy" children . . . to use up time. There are so many better things children can be doing with their time!

In November 1984's issue of *Young Children* (NAEYC), Carol Seefeldt says, "Asking children to complete worksheets may be a form of stealing. Every time children are asked to fill in a worksheet they are being robbed of opportunities to think and learn by doing; experience individualization of instruction; learn to cooperate."

Alternatives to Worksheets

Whenever you are tempted to give children ditto sheets to fill out, ask yourself what purpose you hope to accomplish . . . what skill you were hoping to teach or reinforce with the worksheet. Then ask yourself how else you might give children that experience without using worksheets. Your alternative is bound to be better.

Listed below are a number of typical worksheet "purposes." We'll examine a number of alternative activities that would accomplish the same goals.

1. Visual discrimination exercises, especially to recognize letter and numeral shapes.

e.g.: circle the letter M – H V N M O W

alternatives:

Sorting Activities

Give a child a box of assorted seashells. Pick out one and ask the child to find all the others that are the same kind. Do the same with buttons, socks, nuts, assorted dried beans, etc. (Children must notice details, likenesses and differences.)

Find the Letter

Affix letters or numerals to a table top with clear contact paper. Then hand a child a letter cut-out and let the child find the one that is the same.

Magazine Letter Hunt

Give the child an old magazine and let him cut out examples of the letter or numeral you designate and paste them onto another sheet of paper.

Circle the Letter

Let the child find and circle letters or numerals on a newspaper page. Give the child a magnifying glass to make it more fun.

Letter Sorter

Glue different letters or numerals in sections of egg cartons. Glue matching letters inside bottle caps. The child puts the bottle caps in the egg carton sections with the matching letters or numbers.

2. Associating upper case and lower case letters.

e.g.: draw lines to connect upper and lower case letters:
s d g a k x
G K S D A X
alternatives:

Letter Checkers

Glue upper case letters to squares on a checkerboard. Glue lower case letters to checkers. The child places the checker on the square with the corresponding upper case letter.

Flannel Board Matching

Make felt mushrooms and put upper case letters on them. Put lower case letters on felt snails. Lower case "snails" are matched to upper case "mushrooms."

Let children match upper case and lower case magnetic letters on your magnet board, or felt letters on a flannel board.

3. Associating letters with initial sounds.

e.g.: circle the letter with same beginning sound as "bottle"

D B T G H

alternatives:

Alphabet Clothesline

Attach a clothesline to a wall or divider where children can easily reach it. Put four or five letters on the wall over the clothesline. Have an assortment of objects that represent the letters on the wall with their beginning sounds and some clothespins. The child attaches the object that has the same initial sound under the letter.

Picture Letter Match

Divide a large piece of poster board into a number of squares. Put a different letter in each square. Cut out a picture to represent with its beginning sound each letter on the board. The child must try to place each picture in the correct square.

Gramma's Bag Game

Place several pieces of paper with individual letters written on them on the floor, spread out. In a bag or suitcase, have several objects that represent those letter sounds. Children reach in and take out one object at a time and place it on top of the appropriate letter on the floor.

4. Learning shapes

Shape Hunt

> *Find real objects in the room of the shape you are talking about. ("Plant" some if necessary.)*
> *Use manipulatives or homemade toys that emphasize shape concepts.*

5. To make classroom decorations that go along with a theme unit you are working on with children.

> *If you're learning about airplanes, for instance, visit an airport, and put pictures and books about airplanes in the room for children to see. If they happen to draw airplanes in their spontaneous art work, great. If not, don't worry about it. Coloring in an outline of an airplane will not teach a child a thing about airplanes.*

6. To "test" children to see if they know certain concepts.

> *Simply ask children, or play games such as those just described.*

7. To inform parents about what children are learning.

> *Talk to parents directly. Write notes. At a parent conference or parent night have their own children demonstrate how to play the games. In a parent newsletter, suggest games for parents to play at home with their children that will reinforce concepts being learned at the center.*

Art

Art activities are very popular, and drawings and paintings are often accompanied by stories. The teacher should be ready to take dictation from the child, writing down his words. How wonderful to be able to read words you thought of yourself!

Drawing

Five year olds have "crossed the bridge" from wanting mainly to "mess around" with art materials to wanting to make something recognizable. They will often have an idea ahead of time what they want to draw, and then will go about putting it on paper.

Their people now usually (not always) have a body with limbs, rather than legs and arms coming out of the head. When there is a body, the head still remains relatively large in proportion to the rest of the body.

Children do not need to be taught how to draw. Do not make critical comments about children's representations or try to "correct" the drawing in any way. This type of "instruction" is much more likely to inhibit creativity rather than enhance it.

Concentrate instead on providing children with a wide variety of materials. Expose them to many different art processes. Collage, printing, wax resist, ink, wet chalk, water colors in trays as well as tempera paint, all broaden the child's creative and expressive potential. An art shelf where children can help themselves and carry out their ideas is a real added plus to a kindergarten or pre-kindergarten program.

Collect pictures and books with interesting and beautiful illustrations to develop children's sense of aesthetics. When you select books from the library, look not only for the story matter that will appeal to children. Seek out books with beautiful illustrations.

Science

A very "factual" age, five year olds will enjoy a well-developed science table, and will eagerly learn new words connected with science. They really want to know more about how the world works.

Five year olds will greatly enjoy a wide range of field trips to broaden their understandings. Nature centers, zoos, an auto repair shop, a bakery, are all examples of trips with a science focus that will be interesting to five year olds.

Books about insects, birds, mammals, etc. will be of great interest. Those published by National Geographic are particularly fine. *Ranger Rick* magazine, published by the National Wildlife Federation and *World* magazine, published by National Geographic, provide a wealth of stimulating information.

There are quite a few good teacher resource books on science. One favorite to start with is *Hug a Tree* by Robert E. Rockwell, Elizabeth A. Sherwood, and Robert A. Williams, published by Gryphon House.

Music

Five year olds enjoy all types of music activities. Group singing, dancing, and rhythm band instruments will attract eager participation.

Rhythm Band Orchestra

They can really have fun with rhythm instruments if you show them some different things to do. Try setting them up "orchestra style" with similar instruments grouped together. Then "conduct" them, indicating with your hands when to play loudly and softly, and when certain sections should start and stop. Then, of course, when they get the idea, choose a child to be a conductor.

Math

Many kindergarten programs have some type of structured math program for children. Again, especially for pre-kindergarten children, try to think of alternatives to dittos for learning math concepts.

There are many different processes involved in learning to

understand the system of mathematics. Making and repeating patterns, grouping like objects together into "sets," understanding "one to one correspondence"—touching each object once as you count, rote counting to learn the sequence of numerals, understanding comparisons, sequencing—ordering things from small to large, etc. And we haven't even begun to talk about addition and subtraction.

There is much math you can involve in simple "living" in a classroom. Setting the table, children will have to put down one plate for each child (one to one correspondence) and one fork for each plate, etc. They will have to count how many children are present to know how many plates to get. Are there more children here today than yesterday? How many more?

Making graphs of all types shows children some of the uses of math. How many people have blue eyes in our class? How many have brown eyes? Green eyes? Put these on a graph and then compare the numbers. Which line has most . . . which least? Make graphs about the weather, about what kinds of pets kids have, about favorite musicians, about how many buttons people have on their clothes that day, about their favorite flavor ice cream, etc., etc., etc.

Time

Five year olds understand most of the abstract concepts of space and time. They know the days of the week, the months, the season.

This is the ideal age to do "calendar activities," reinforcing names of days and months, counting, and experiencing left to right progression. It's also a good context for learning ordinal numbers . . . first, second, third, etc.

They also benefit from playing with hour glasses, egg timers, and stop watches.

Cooking projects give children many practical experiences with mathematics.

Most five year olds cannot tell time except in a rudimentary way.

Focus

The obvious focus of kindergarten and pre-kindergarten programs is "getting ready for school." Don't let your focus on the future ignore the child as he is today. Keep your programs fun.

Five year olds like to know a lot of facts. Their "why" and "how" questions are legitimate requests for knowledge. Expand their world, building in as many new experiences as you can.

CHAPTER 9

Six, Seven And Eight Year Olds

These are known as the "middle years," or "early middle years." These children are industrious. They like to make things, compete with each other, and against themselves, and do real work using real tools. It is during these years that most societies start children in formal schooling or training for later adult roles. Many child care programs care for children of this age after school and during the summer. However, if these children are treated the same as preschool children, we're headed for trouble. Their interests and needs are different, which requires a different approach to supervising, teaching and entertaining them.

People who work with middle years kids need to be flexible, energetic, resourceful, and interested . . . an organizer, a teacher of skills, a friend. Some programs stress outdoor activities and sports, while others stress crafts and making things. A balance of both is ideal. A sense of humor doesn't hurt!

Physical

Children this age are growing and developing physical skills rapidly, although the rate of growth has slowed down a bit in comparison to the preschool years.

Developing skills and "gaining mastery" are dominant drives of the school-ager. A yearning for competence combines itself with industriousness. Skill building activities of all types are popular; all kinds of sports, games such as jacks, hula hoops, jump rope, playing musical instruments, developing skill in a craft such as knitting and macrame are examples of this drive. Learning sign language has been a favorite activity of some school-age programs.

Their ability to acquire such new physical skills can also be closely connected with their development of self-esteem. Feeling capable in physical skills relates directly to a child's self concept. Some children are quite good at physical tasks, and learn easily. Others may be awkward and clumsy due to uneven physical growth. For this reason, it is important for a caregiver to try to help each child gain skills, or find an activity at which she or he can excel. A child who may be poor at ball playing could be an excellent swimmer, or very good at needlepoint.

Risks

These children like to test their abilities, take risks, show off and dare each other in a show of bravado. For this reason, even though they may seem very capable, they still require supervision and an occasional adult-imposed limit. Make sure playground equipment is kept in good repair.

While remaining responsible for children's safety in a child care situation, we can provide them with "safe" risks. Performing in front of their peers is one good way. Dramatic skits, talent shows, comedic routines, etc. are popular activities.

Energy

Children this age are typically very energetic and enjoy strenuous physical activity. Do take care to provide a balance in the day. Children who have been cooped up in a very structured school situation all day will need to blow off steam and run and yell when they first arrive in the afternoon. On the other hand, a full day program, on vacations, will need a balance of quiet time.

Food

School-age kids always seem to be hungry. It would be wise to acknowledge and anticipate this. Provide generous and nourishing snacks and lots to drink. The afternoon will go much more smoothly and everyone will be in a better mood if you remember this. This is one reason cooking projects are very popular in many school-age programs.

Social

Relationships to Adults

The relationship to the adult in charge is different for school-agers than it was for preschool children. Younger children have great emotional dependence on their caregiver and the majority of their interactions are with the caregiver. With older children, the role of the adult is less central in the child's interactions. Instead of looking to the adult for gratification, school-aged children look to each other. The role of the adult must shift accordingly from one of nurturer and entertainer to one of facilitator and supporter. The adult should work with kids planning what would be fun and help them get the materials they need. Arrange time and space to give children a wide choice of activities. "Be there" for children, to act in a supportive role in children's problem-solving and conflict resolution processes.

Peers

The peer group emerges as supreme at this age. Interaction with friends of about the same age takes on significant importance for the child. Caregivers must realize that some children will do almost anything to gain the acceptance of other children.

Contact with other children of the same age allows for the give and take experiences that allow children to develop their own personal styles and personalities. Caregivers can help see that the impact of a peer group is a positive one. Helping a child gain acceptance and feel like an important part of the group is an important focus for the caregiver. There are things you can do to help assure that each child has friends.

1. Model being a good friend yourself. Give each child a friendly greeting and make time to talk to kids individually, just asking about school, and what's going on in their lives. Be interested, without being judgmental. Although children will enjoy some kidding or teasing, remain sensitive, and keep sarcasm out of your interactions. If other kids sense that *you* like a person, they are more likely to be friendly toward that person themselves.

2. You can plan activities that are comfortably done in a small social group. Let children choose many of their own activities, and with whom they will do them much of the time. You can, however, "engineer" certain relationships, setting an activity up so that two children do something together and get acquainted in the process.

3. You may be able to help children gain social skills by "coaching" in certain situations.

Children between the ages of six and eight usually choose to play with someone of their own sex. This is by no means rigid. Boys seem more preoccupied with the "male role" than girls are with the "feminine role." Try to keep gender stereotyping out of your activities. Recognize that boys may enjoy jewelry making and cooking and girls will enjoy carpentry and playing ball. Keep activities open to both sexes.

Solitude

Children this age may also need some time to get away from the gang and be by themselves. Is there a closet in your room you could fix up with a light, a rug and some pillows where a child could be permitted to go by himself? Perhaps you could rig up some "one-person" corners in your room using large boxes or furniture to block off a small corner. After all, they've been with other people all day. A little solitude might present some needed relief. Some children need this more than others.

Clubs

Middle years children like to form cliques and clubs with their peers. Groups such as this are constantly forming and reforming. Kids often spend more time organizing the club and discussing rules, roles, and the status of individual members than they do actually doing anything. The guidance of an adult can turn the negative aspects of cliques into the positive aspects of clubs and give clubs the means and subtle direction to actually accomplish something as well. This is probably one reason for the traditional success of scouting programs for this age. Some successful school-age child care programs take advantage of this interest and are organized as "clubs" with "governments." This can work really well if the adult acts as the "advisor" and not the leader of the whole operation. Allow the kids to think of their own roles, rules, and procedures. Most important, let them plan activities they would like to do. It is a good idea to encourage frequent "re-elections" to allow different children to try different roles and experience leadership.

Help children gain a sense of identity with their "club." Uniforms served this function for scouts. Perhaps you can decorate your own club T-shirts. Club handshakes, secret pass words, codes, etc. help accomplish this goal. The end result is a feeling of belonging.

Children can be divided into smaller "sub-groups" from time to time, perhaps as a way for signing up for a special activity. Try forming a needlepoint club or a cooking club which a limited number can sign up for that will be in existence for a few weeks while new skills are learned.

Rules

School-aged children are "rule-bound." Their concept of justice is black and white, not abstract and flexible.

Children should be involved in setting rules for the classroom and its various procedures and routines. The teacher will have to ensure that rules remain simple, fair, enforceable and consistent because children often become carried away and harsh in their rules and punishments when left to their own devices.

Games with rules are very popular. Whether they are board games, card games, word games, or active games, kids enjoy competing in this way. Try getting kids to make up their own games and rules for them. Rules can be discussed and changed with consensus of the group.

Competition

Competition is a fact of life for this age, like it or not. Children are always comparing how their work or skill stands up compared to someone else's. They like to win. You will not eliminate competition by banning games or sports. The adult *can* have a significant influence on how kids take winning and losing. Giving praise for a "good try" or a "game well-played" as well as for winning can have a positive effect on how kids feel about themselves. The adult can also moderate the behavior of winners. It's OK to feel good about it, but not to lord it over everyone else in a braggadocio way.

Kids also enjoy competing against themselves, and "setting personal records." Providing timers and stop watches give opportunities to compete with themselves, and can add new challenges to mundane activities.

One good book of games enjoyed by middle years children is *The Outrageous Outdoor Games Book*, by Bob Gregson, Pitman Learning, Inc.

Autonomy

Children this age like to do things by themselves and manage themselves from time to time. This is an important need to take into consideration. Giving kids lots of choices of possible things to do, letting them structure their own time, decide what they want to do, form their own groups, initiate activities teachers didn't suggest, and take an active part in planning classroom activities and routines help accommodate this need. Important here is allowing a child to choose *not* to do an activity that is offered. Kids who are over-supervised, directed too closely, "dominated" by the teacher, will rebel.

Fairness

"Fairness" is a major preoccupation of this age group. "Fair" means "equal" to them. Everyone should get the same amount, and be treated the same, according to their thinking.

Conflict Resolution

Many caregivers of this age list "discipline" as one of the more difficult aspects of working with this age. "Discipline" is an ambiguous word with many meanings. What caregivers are usually talking about is helping children get along with each other in a way that takes the rights and feelings of others into consideration.

At the top of the list is dealing with aggression. As discussed above, kids this age have a very narrow understanding of "fairness." That understanding drives them to "even the score." Many fights occur when one child tries to "get even" with another child for something done to them. Furthermore, they sometimes do not understand the accidental nature of some aggression. Say one child does a somersault and accidently kicks a second child. The second child may have a strong desire to hit or otherwise hurt the somersaulter, even though it was an accident. It helps to teach kids to say quickly, "I didn't mean to hurt you . . . it was an accident." It may also help "even the score" if you can get the person who committed the accident or aggression to help the victim. Getting the victim a cold cloth, or helping rebuild or remake something destroyed could help.

Industriousness

Children this age have been characterized as "industrious." They are very busy learning new skills, making things, "doing stuff."

They need to feel the purposefulness of what they are doing. In sharp contrast to preschoolers, who often have very little interest in the final product of their art work, school-agers are very interested in achieving an acceptable final product for their efforts. "Making things" is very important. They also don't mind stretching a project over several days in order to complete it as long as the product is satisfying. Therefore, such projects as woodworking, papier mache, ceramics, puppet making and weaving are greatly enjoyed.

They do demonstrate a real need to complete their projects and get very discouraged if things must be left undone. It helps if teachers break down large projects that will take several days to complete into smaller tasks that can be completed in one day. Thus kids will have a feeling of satisfaction at accomplishing something, even though the whole project isn't done yet. For instance, making a papier mache dragon could take weeks. The teacher could say, "Today we want to put on one whole layer of papier mache that will cover the whole body." Or, "Today we will paint the head." Or for a needlepoint pillow, give the child a goal of 3 rows, and congratulate for accomplishing that target goal.

School-agers also need to feel that what they do is needed and important. They like to use real tools and equipment rather than toys, to do real work and help in real ways. Cooking, woodworking, painting, helping with office work, helping other teachers with such things as bulletin boards, even janitorial activities appeal. They are especially responsive when adults express sincere appreciation.

Collections

List making and collecting things are popular activities. Trading cards, matchbox cars, marbles, rock collections, stamp collections, taking surveys, opinion polls, making a record, compiling data—are all activities that are likely to appeal to six to eight year olds.

Tournaments are a type of collection. Children play a game over and over, trying to see how many points they can rack up over a period of time.

Summary

Although there are many models of child care programs for children ages six through eight, most successful programs have several things in common.

1. Recognizing the importance of the peer group, a "group identity" is established. The group often has a special name, passwords, etc. and an organization that allows different children to

take on leadership roles from time to time. Children have a big say in planning what the group will do and in carrying out projects.

2. Rather than being a "teacher" in the traditional sense of the word, adults are a combination facilitator, arbitrator, and friend. They are there to help children solve their own problems, get the materials needed to carry out plans, and have a good time with kids.

3. Rules are kept to a minimum, but are consistently enforced.

4. There is opportunity for sports and games allowing children to compete with each other and learn new skills. Competition is handled lightly, with large doses of encouragement.

5. Children are given many opportunities to make things in crafts of all types.

There are plenty of things to do, and children are allowed to choose what they would like to do or *not* do.

Bibliography

Developmental Discussions

Ames, Louise Bates, and Ilg, Frances: *Your One Year Old, Your Two Year Old, Your Three Year Old, Your Four Year Old, Your Five Year Old.* Dell Publishing Company, 245 E. 47th St., New York, NY 10010
   These books, written for parents, are easy reading with very useful descriptions of children at various stages.

Bender, Judith, Flatter, Charles H. and Schuyler-Hass, Barbara Elder: *Half a Childhood,* 1984. School Age Notes, P.O. Box 120674, Nashville, TN 37212
   A discussion of child care for school age children—its administration, funding and organization as well as the developmental characteristics of children 5 through 12, and program designs and activities that work well with this age group. An extremely helpful book.

Lansky, Vicki: *Toilet Training,* Practical Parenting Press.
   A thorough discussion of the topic with many practical tips.

Le Shan, Eda: *Conspiracy Against Childhood,* 1974. Atheneum, 597 Fifth Avenue, New York, NY 10017
   This book addresses the problems of parents who want to push children to learn skills before they are ready, robbing them of valuable play time in the early childhood years.

151

Miller, Karen: *Things To Do With Toddlers and Twos,* 1984. Tel-
    share Publishing Co., Inc. P.O. Box 679, Marshfield, MA 02050
        A collection of over 400 activities that work well with this
    age group. Developmental discussions are connected to the
    activities.

Mitchell, Grace: *A Very Practical Guide to Discipline With Young
    Children,* 1982. Telshare Publishing Co., Inc. P.O. Box 679,
    Marshfield, MA 02050
        This easy to read book describes many typical behavior prob-
    lems of children of all ages, and gives adults possible solutions
    that preserve the dignity of both parties.

White, Burton: *The First Three Years of Life.*
    Avon Publishers, 1790 Broadway, New York, NY 10019
        This book has very helpful descriptions of the stages of
    infancy and toddlerhood.

Curriculum Resources

Conn Beall, Pamela and Hagan Nipp, Susan: *Wee Sing, Wee Sing
    and Play,* and *Wee Sing Silly Songs.* Price/Stern/Sloan Pub-
    lishers, 410 N. La Cienega Blvd., Los Angeles, CA 90048
        Great for three years old and older, these three little books
    have all the old favorites for which you've forgotten the words.

Warren, Jean: *Piggyback Songs for Infants and Toddlers.* Warren
    Publishing Co., 2240 Galahad Drive, Indianapolis, IN 46208
        Here's a book which will make it easy for the teacher who
    cannot read music to involve singing in her everyday routines.

Periodicals

Beginnings, P.O. Box 2890, Redmond, WA 98052
        This publication, written specifically for child care staff,
    discusses critical issues of child care, focusing on a different
    topic in each issue. Infants and toddlers are discussed in rela-
    tion to the given topic in each issue.

Caring for Infants and Toddlers. Resources for Child Care Man-
    agement, P.O. Box 669, Summit, NJ 07901
        A bi-monthly newsletter focused on child care in the first

two years. It involves thoughtful discussions of research per-
taining to practice in caring for infants and toddlers, as well as
many practical tips.

School Age Notes, P.O. Box 120674, Nashville, TN 37212
    This is a publication dealing specifically with child care
programs for children between 5 and 12. It describes many
activities enjoyed by this age group and with a focus on the
developmental characteristics of school agers. There is always
a page on "conflict resolution" dealing with typical discipline
problems and possible solutions.